More Acclaim for *Crashing the Gate*

"There is a new politics being born in America that isn't beholden to the rich, the dishonest, and the corrupt. *Crashing the Gate* shows how that politics has emerged, and how it is bringing power back to the people. This is a book that the political establishment will likely fear—but only because it proves that ordinary citizens are ready to take back their government."

—David Sirota, author of *Hostile Takeover: How Big Money & Corruption Conquered Our Government & How We Take It Back*

"True to their calling, Armstrong and Moulitsas—masters of the blog—provide a no-holds-barred overview of the political landscape. If you want to know why blogs have become crucial to the re-establishment of American democracy, read this book."

—George Lakoff, author of *Don't Think of an Elephant!*

"The political status quo isn't working, and Markos and Jerome finally tell it like it is. More importantly they offer every frustrated citizen a way out. Calling on 'regular people' to become 'the financial backbone of the Democratic Party,' *Crashing the Gate* offers both the historical perspective needed to recognize that each of us must rise to this challenge to build a political future we can live with and the path to do it."

—Kirstin Falk, executive director of the New Progressive Coalition

"This 'simple' book may be one of the most important that has come out of the progressive movement in over a decade."

—Aaron Barlow, ePluribus Media

"This book isn't meant to be read and pondered; it's meant to be provocative, talked about, and argued over. It's meant to create that sense of 'us' that's been missing from the party for so long. It's meant to have us Democrats . . . talking about *our* party, the real party of the people."

—Matt Stoller, political blogger

"*Crashing the Gate* impels us to leave behind the hollow comfort of our individual organizations and unite to build the people-powered movement that our democracy so desperately needs. Let the reformation begin!"

—Jared Duval, national director of the Sierra Student Coalition

NETROOTS, GRASSROOTS, AND THE RISE OF PEOPLE-POWERED POLITICS

Jerome Armstrong
Markos Moulitsas Zúniga

Foreword by Simon Rosenberg

CHELSEA GREEN PUBLISHING COMPANY
WHITE RIVER JUNCTION, VERMONT

Managing Editor: Marcy Brant
Editor: Safir Ahmed
Copy Editor: Cannon Labrie
Designer: Peter Holm, Sterling Hill Productions
Design Assistant: Daria Hoak, Sterling Hill Productions
Indexer: Peggy Holloway

Printed in the United States
First printing, February 2006
10 9 8 7 6 5 4 3 2 1

Our Commitment to Green Publishing

Chelsea Green sees publishing as a tool for cultural change and ecological stewardship.
We strive to align our book manufacturing practices with our editorial mission, and to
reduce the impact of our business enterprise on the environment. We print our books
and catalogs on chlorine-free recycled paper, using soy-based inks, whenever possible.
Chelsea Green is a member of the Green Press Initiative (www.greenpressinitiative.org),
a nonprofit coalition of publishers, manufacturers, and authors working to protect the
world's endangered forests and conserve natural resources. *Crashing the Gate* was printed
on Ecobook 100 Natural, a 100 percent post-consumer-waste recycled, old-growth-
forest-free paper supplied by New Leaf.

Library of Congress Cataloging-in-Publication Data

Armstrong, Jerome, 1964-
   Crashing the gate : Netroots, grassroots, and the rise of people-powered
politics / Jerome Armstrong, Markos Moulitsas Zúniga.
       p. cm.
   Includes bibliographical references and index.
   ISBN-13 978-1-931498-99-9
   ISBN-10 1-931498-99-7
   1. Politics, Practical—United States. 2. United States—Politics and
government—2001- 3. Weblogs—Political aspects—United States. I.
Moulitsas Zúniga, Markos, 1971- II. Title.
   JK1764.A76 2005
   324.70973—dc22
                                        2005036402
Chelsea Green Publishing Company
Post Office Box 428
White River Junction, VT 05001
(800) 639-4099
www.chelseagreen.com

"First they ignore you, then they laugh at you,
then they fight you, then you win."

Mahatma Gandhi

CONTENTS

FOREWORD

When Jerome and Markos asked me to write this foreword, I was both honored and surprised. While we had collaborated, supped, and fought together, we did not approach our political work from the same place. They opposed the Iraq War; I supported it. They were an important part of Howard Dean's transformative campaign; I admired their work but did not support the governor's presidential primary run. They are new to the political arena; I've been working in national politics and media for twenty years.

But after mulling it over I decided to write this foreword for three reasons.

First, Jerome and Markos share my sense of urgency about creating a new politics for progressives, one suited to the challenges and opportunities of our time. They know that the twentieth-century progressivism that dominated American politics was a tremendous success—it fostered a stable world and a prosperous America, while supporting the labor, civil rights, environmental, women's rights, consumer, and other social change movements that made our great nation stronger and more just.

When last in control of the federal government, Democrats demonstrated the power of effective, progressive governance. Under President Bill Clinton's administration, we saw the largest peacetime economic expansion in our nation's history, producing 22 million new jobs, higher incomes for many Americans, a decline in poverty, and a radical shift in the national budget from historic deficits to unprecedented surpluses. We reformed welfare, embraced the digital revolution and globalization, invested in public schools, expanded health-care coverage to millions more children, and fought for universal, high-quality, affordable health care for every American. Thanks to a tough but compassionate American foreign policy, the world remained at peace, as we worked with our allies to unite people and nations around common challenges. It is a record to be proud of.

But this politics of progress is no longer dominant, having been challenged by an ascendant Republican Party and conservative movement. Democrats controlled much of the federal government for most of the last seventy years of the twentieth century. In recent years, fueled by billions of dollars of investment in a very modern political machine, these Republicans and movement conservatives have seized Washington and displaced the Democrats, and they now have more control than at any time since the 1920s.

Driving the sense of urgency felt by many is what has happened to America since President Bush and these new conservatives came to power. Guided by an ideological approach to governing developed in a long political exile, modern conservatives are long on sales and marketing and short on effective governance.

At home, they've turned record budget surpluses into staggering deficits. The average family has seen its wages decline while shouldering a greater share of the overall tax burden. Personal bankruptcies, health care costs, college tuition, energy bills and the number of uninsured and poor Americans all continue to rise. The president has shorted his signature education reform effort by over $30 billion, leaving millions of children behind. Under this regime, capital and corporations have prospered, but the American people and their government have not.

Meanwhile, these new conservatives ignored warnings about the growing power of Al-Qaeda, leaving America vulnerable to attack. The new Department of Homeland Security has received failing grades, Hurricane Katrina demonstrated the degree to which we are ill-prepared for national emergencies, and Osama bin Laden roams free. They launched a war on Iraq based on lies and were terribly unprepared to finish the job they started. They have unnecessarily cost Americans our prestige around the world, billions of taxpayer dollars, and thousands of lives. The president's go-it-alone foreign policy has weakened international institutions critical to tackling common global challenges. In this new era America has become less safe.

Of all the ways modern conservatives have let America down, there is perhaps no greater example or more profound moral failure than the manner in which they have so quickly become corrupted by the power they had sought for so long and have had so briefly. As of this writing, the Department of Justice is conducting criminal investigations deep into the Bush administration, the Senate, the House, and the conservative leadership, uncovering breathtaking abuses of power, illegal activity, and corruption.

All of this has weakened our great country, leaving our people less prosperous, less safe, and less free and our government mired in one of the most extraordinary sets of scandals in American history.

Jerome and Markos understand that as proud and patriotic Americans it is their duty to challenge progressives to reject this unacceptable new conservative era. They have, through their blogs, become important leaders in helping America find a new and better path.

My second reason is that Jerome and Markos have been pioneers in helping progressives master new technologies and new media. As they write so effectively, the twentieth-century ways in which we communicated with one another were largely broadcast—centralized television and radio stations beaming out messages to vast audiences. The communications media of this new century are something else entirely—more iterative, more participatory, more transparent, more personal, more honest, more one-to-one, more global, and more *democratic*. In this technology-driven era, people are less passive consumers and more active participants.

Blogs like MyDD and Daily Kos have helped create and fuel this new politics. Led by regular people, not political insiders, the blogosphere has brought the great debate that is our democracy to millions of citizens hungry for a more meaningful way to participate in our politics. Unprecedented numbers of Americans now plug into a conversation, a community, 24/7/365, from wherever they are—from their offices, their homes, their local libraries. Extrapolating from a report the New Politics Institute released in the summer of 2005, the progressive blogosphere is now reaching more Americans than such progressive stalwarts as the DNC, MoveOn, Air America and the Sierra Club. Daily Kos itself has more readers than the four big left-of-center newsmagazines—*The American Prospect, The Nation, The New Republic* and the *Washington Monthly*—combined.

We saw the impact of this new era in the last presidential election cycle. Record numbers of people participated in the political debate, volunteered, contributed money, and voted. As the party of the people, Democrats should understand and embrace the new technologies and media that allow millions of regular people to join our fight.

As with most things connected to the internet and new media, however, this new politics is disruptive, upsetting old arrangements and displacing people invested in the old ways. It is literally "crashing the gate" of the old system, as Jerome and Markos say. And to that I say, "Amen." For progressives, our essential mission these days is to honor and learn from our proud past, and set about the business of forging a twenty-first-century movement suited to the new challenges and realities. The blogosphere is an essential part of this effort, as it has brought people, passion, innovation, experimentation, and debate back into our politics—necessary ingredients all, if we are to triumph in the years ahead.

My third reason is that I have come to like and admire Jerome and Markos. As concerned Americans, they jumped off the sidelines and plunged into the political arena. They bared their souls, took their lumps, and made their case. They have repeatedly shown courage and grit. We disagree on some important issues, but I recognize leadership when I see it, and these two guys have been vital, important leaders for progressives in a very dark and difficult period for our politics.

At a critical point in my own life I made a similar leap. I was in college during Ronald Reagan's first term in the White House, and saw the way the conservatives were effectively challenging our approach. I learned a lot about the American people and Democratic politics traveling the country for Michael Dukakis's presidential campaign in 1988, and spent five years writing and producing television news shows and documentaries in New York. But in late 1991, some friends introduced me to Bill Clinton, then a young, dynamic governor from Arkansas, and my life changed for good. I joined that inspiring campaign and became a part of a modernizing movement—the New Democrats—which helped us win two consecutive presidential elections for the first time in thirty years, and which produced a government that left America better and stronger than before.

My work, since I joined politics full-time in 1992, has been to modernize progressive politics, helping our proud movement adapt to new and changing circumstances. That quest led me to build the organization I run today, NDN, and its think tank, the New Politics Institute. And all these years of success and failure, trial and error, have made me conclude that if we really want to build a modern movement, then progressives of all stripes and flavors, and from all regions of the country, must learn to work together, to tolerate and respect our differences, to debate but not to fight, to understand that we are all playing different positions on the same team.

So in that spirit, I am excited and proud to stand with Jerome and Markos as they offer a provocative early draft of the new history of progressive politics, and I look forward to working with them for many years in our vital efforts to restore the promise of our great nation.

SIMON ROSENBERG

PREFACE

Five years ago, the Republicans took over the government through nondemocratic means. Establishment Democrats, for the most part, stood back and watched as a partisan judicial body halted the counting of presidential votes. While conservative activists led the charge on behalf of their party, there was nothing happening on our side. That was the spark. Fed-up progressive activists began organizing online. Fueled by the new technologies—the web, blogging tools, internet search engines—this new generation of activists challenged the moribund Democratic Party establishment. We didn't have the money, the connections, or the pedigree to break into the insular world of traditional politics. But in the democratic world of online activism, we didn't need those things to be heard.

Both of us started our blogs because we wanted a voice in our nation's politics. We had hundreds, then thousands, of readers, as we somehow tapped into a greater need for strong progressive voices—voices that had been shut out of the corporate media outlets. And the online medium allowed a level of participation nonexistent in traditional media. It wasn't us talking down to our readers. It was all of us collectively having a conversation.

Our sites grew in size and influence. Daily Kos is now the largest political blog in the world by a factor of three or four. Jerome's MyDD is one of the most influential political blogs in the nation. We were present at the birth of the online efforts of both the Howard Dean and Wesley Clark presidential campaigns. We had the type of access that most journalists would kill for, and our obsessive hour-to-hour coverage of the political scene gave us knowledge and perspective completely absent from the traditional media. Thus, we ended up with a front-row seat for the amazing changes in the political landscape over the past four years. We suppose it was inevitable that we would end up chronicling those changes.

Many people wanted us to write a book about blogging, but that seemed too self-indulgent for our tastes. Moreover, blogging is simply the medium; what we blog *about* is politics. In the past five years, we watched Republicans crush Democrats in election after election, and we wanted to do something about it. But first, we wanted to figure out *why* Democrats were on such a losing streak and *how* that could be changed.

In May 2005 we began traveling all over the country to interview political insiders and outsiders—journalists, politicians, consultants, historians, authors, and activists. We traveled to over twenty states and interviewed over 150 people. We had an early thesis—that the Democratic Party's biggest problem was "branding," or rather the lack of it. However, that thesis was decimated by the research and interviews during our travels. (Suffice it to say, the party has bigger problems than branding or marketing.) We wanted to write a book with intellectual heft, but we are neither historians nor political scientists. Our underqualified efforts to write heavy political and historical material failed miserably.

By late August 2005 we were at a cabin in Whitefish, Montana, with the first draft of the book due in a mere five weeks. We'd planned the Montana retreat months in advance to wrap up the book, yet we found ourselves scrapping all that we had written and starting from scratch. Our editor, Safir Ahmed, joined us a couple of days into the weeklong retreat and did a great job of hiding the panic that was inevitably there.

Perhaps it was the good beer and wine, or the view of gorgeous Whitefish Lake, or the shock of the Hurricane Katrina disaster that week and George W. Bush's incompetent response. Whatever it was, as we talked about what we had really learned from our research, interviews, and our experiences, inspiration struck. We are part of a new, nationwide, reform-minded progressive movement that is both populist and patriotic at heart and that is already changing the political, media, and activism landscapes in profound and long-lasting ways. This book tells that story. Halfway through this decade, it's still just beginning.

JEROME ARMSTRONG
Alexandria, Virginia

MARKOS MOULITSAS
Berkeley, California

January 2006

AMERICAN REALITY, CIRCA 2006

**"This country is going so far to the right
that you won't recognize it."**
—Hunter S. Thompson,
Fear and Loathing: On the Campaign Trail '72

"Hey, hey, ho, ho, Social Security has got to go!"
—College Republicans' chant at a campaign
event for Senator Rick Santorum, February 2005

We have a Republican Party that can't govern, a Democratic Party that can't get elected, and little doubt that a great nation is suffering as a result.

A prescient headline in the satirical publication *The Onion* proclaimed three days before George W. Bush's inauguration as the nation's forty-third president on January 20, 2001: "Bush: 'Our Long National Nightmare of Peace and Prosperity Is Finally Over.'" While some took solace in the fact that Bush actually lost the popular vote and stole the election in 2000, the results were much harder to explain away in 2004. Bush's first term was a disaster, both on the domestic and foreign policy fronts. Nevertheless, the American people hit the polls on November 2, 2004, and delivered a legitimate victory to the very architect of the nation's greatest woes. It was a stunning rejection of the Democratic Party and an undeserved validation of a Republican Party that has been hijacked by ideologues who place their dogma above the national interest.

Meanwhile, we've also been plagued by a Democratic Party unsure of itself, lacking the expression of any core principles, and devoid of any institutional machinery to develop and promote its agenda. Democrats have utterly failed to offer a compelling alternative to Bush and his Republican acolytes, oftentimes parroting Republican positions on any number of issues in the mistaken belief that it might help them capture centrist or independent voters. We saw that strategy fail in 2000, in 2002, and in 2004. But the Democratic Party—its leadership in Washington, D.C., its legions of campaign consultants and the single-issue groups that form its traditional base—has failed to learn lessons from these recurring losses. The party's stakeholders resist being dislodged from their entrenched positions of wealth and power. Even as a marginalized minority, they won't surrender their fiefdoms without a fight. Why risk their comfy little gigs and rackets in a bid for majority status when they've already got it so good?

The Democrats are content to wait for the Republicans to self-destruct so that they can become the default option. Sure, the ever-increasing scandals and mismanagement surrounding the Republican Party threaten to drown its near-term electoral chances. But Democrats can't be political vultures—winning only when there are rotting Republican carcasses to munch on. We need a party that can win on the strength of its own ideas and convictions. And we need to build our forces to match what the Republicans have on the political battlefield—in technology usage, in media access and resources, in research and message development, and in training and leadership efforts.

We cannot wait any longer for the Democratic Party to reform itself and lead us into a new era of electoral success. Those of us who became energized ever since Bush and his circle of fiends took over in 2000—the netroots, the grassroots, the *progressive base* of America—must act now to take back our party and our country. They may view us in D.C. as barbarians at the gate, but we are not armed with pitchforks and torches. Technology has opened up the previously closed realm of activist politics to riffraff like us. Whether the stagnant establishment wants it or not, the new progressive populist movement will reclaim the Democratic Party as the party of the people. Our message is simple: You can get out of the way or work with us. Trying to stop us is a losing proposition.

If only we could say, "To hell with the Democratic Party!" But part of the present American reality is that we live in a two-party system, and the Democratic Party is our only alternative. It's efficient—and expedient—to reform the existing party of the left, much as the conservative movement took over the Republican Party in the 1970s and converted it into the electoral powerhouse it is today.

Time is of the essence. America is going to hell in a handbasket under a morally and economically bankrupt Republican leadership. We need an authentic and populist democratic movement to crash the gate and save our nation.

Some political observers claim that unlike a generation ago, the United States is now a conservative nation, that Republicans are now the dominant governing party. And given recent Republican successes, it's certainly plausible. The Republicans own the government, controlling the White House, Congress, the Supreme Court, and an increasing number of federal benches that will block progressive policies for the next thirty to forty years. Republicans and their powerful machine have taken aim at every single cause progressives hold dear and have undone whatever progress had been achieved. They annihilated the gun control groups, beat the labor movement down to a shadow of its former self, weakened the pro-choice groups, took shots at the trial lawyers, watered down the gains of the environmental movement, and diverted public resources for the low and middle classes to their wealthy corporate cronies. To keep winning at the ballot box, however, Republicans would have to show an ability to govern. And given their performance these past five years, their inability to run the country and meet the needs of all Americans (not just the rich and the corporations) will be their undoing.

In this decade, Republicans have turned President Bill Clinton's record surpluses into record deficits, dismantled environmental protections on behalf of their corporate patrons, and mired us in a deadly and costly quagmire in Iraq. They have helped export millions of jobs overseas, have forced formerly well-paid workers into the low-pay, low-benefits Wal-Mart economy, and have created a big-government bureaucratic mess out of our public education system. Meanwhile, they have done nothing to improve the health-care system as millions more Americans go without health insurance and access to decent medical care. To top it all off, the Bush administration and its Wall Street cohorts have set their sights on destroying the single most popular government program in the nation's history—Social Security.

By any measure, the Republican agenda is not America's agenda. It is the agenda of some of the major groups of conservatives—or cons—of the Republican Party.

THE CORPORATE CONS

Joe Allbaugh was a central figure in Bush's rise to power, playing the role of "enforcer" during Bush's campaigns and as his chief of staff in Texas. He has always been known as one of Bush's most trusted aides, along with Karl Rove and Karen Hughes. He ran the Bush-Cheney campaign in 2000. After the Supreme Court appointed Bush to the White House in January 2001, Bush appointed Allbaugh to head the Federal Emergency Management Agency (FEMA). His two-year tenure as FEMA director was rife with allegations of massive fraud in the agency's contracting. In March 2003, Allbaugh left FEMA and teamed up with cronies of Haley Barbour, the former chairman of the Republican National Committee and current governor of Mississippi, to form a private company named New Bridge Strategies LLC—just in time to take advantage of the Iraq War. The new firm's specialty was shaking down lucrative reconstruction contracts in Iraq. Or as Allbaugh puts it on his company's website:

> New Bridge Strategies, LLC, is a unique company that was created specifically with the aim of assisting clients to evaluate and take advantage of business opportunities in the Middle East following the conclusion of the U.S.-led war in Iraq. . . . The opportunities evolving in Iraq today are of such an unprecedented nature and scope that companies seeking to work in that environment must have the very best advice and guidance available.

In March 2005, Allbaugh signed on to work for Halliburton "to educate the congressional and executive branch on defense, disaster relief and homeland security issues."[1] Immediately after Hurricane Katrina hit the Gulf Coast in late August, Allbaugh headed down to help "coordinate the private-sector response to the storm," which is apparently a polite way to say he was "bring[ing] his influence peddling racket" to the region (as blogger Josh Marshall put it). Sure enough, first in line to benefit from the human tragedy in New Orleans was none other than Halliburton,[2] helped, no doubt, by the fact that Allbaugh had signed on as a lobbyist for the company.

Let's summarize: We have the president and vice president's former campaign manager and confidant appointed to head the disaster-management agency who is now reaping profits from "business opportunities" created by the president's war on Iraq and from "business opportunities" _he_ created for the vice president's former company following the Katrina disaster.

It's all par for the course for the corporate conservative—the oldest of the Republican constituency groups. Corporate cons seek to craft a government friendly to unfettered, unregulated capitalism, not to mention a government that provides generous subsidies and a steady stream of lucrative contracts to further line their pockets—codifying the culture of corruption into the nation's laws. This faction is the granddaddy of the Republican Party—the oil barons, the railroad tycoons, the steel magnates, all grown fat on corporate welfare, growing even fatter under the Bush administration. For the corporate cons, if Halliburton, Shell, and Texaco are enjoying all-time high profits, then it's time for them to get more tax breaks under the new energy bill—the same bill crafted in secret by Vice President Dick Cheney and energy industry executives in May 2001. By the time Bush signed the bill into law in August 2005, it contained $14.5 billion in tax breaks, mostly for the large energy companies.

There is nothing inherently bad about big business, but the corporate cons put their financial profits ahead of the national interest. Much like the corporate boardrooms they occupy, they run their government behind closed doors, away from the prying eyes of the media and public. They dole out their no-bid contracts among friends, all the while treating the public's "right to know" as an unwelcome nuisance. Regulatory agencies are infested with insiders from the very industries those agencies are supposed to regulate, encouraging a "fox in the henhouse" atmosphere.

They sure take care of their own. The pharmaceutical industry, which pumped more than $50 million into the campaign coffers of Bush and other Republicans between 1999 and 2003, gained a handsome reward with the passage of the Medicare prescription drug bill in 2003. The *Boston Globe* reported in October 2004 that estimates for increase in drug-industry revenues from the bill ranged between $100 billion and $139 billion over the first eight years beginning in 2006. That's a nice return on that $50 million investment in the Republican Party. Among other things, the bill prevents Medicare from even negotiating volume discounts from Big Pharma when it buys drugs for its forty million beneficiaries.

Down in the states, the corporate cons have had a little run of bad luck lately. In Ohio, the cons funneled $50 million of workers' compensation dollars to a party donor who "invested" it in rare coins and stamps. The ensuing scandal, in which $10–$12 million came up missing, has rocked the Ohio Republican establishment. In Texas, Travis County District Attorney Ronnie Earle has been on an indictment binge of House Majority Leader Tom DeLay's circle and his political action committee, Texans for a Republican Majority, which solicited illegal corporate donations to take over the state legislature and redraw the Texas congressional map. One of the corporate donors, Weststar Energy, gave a $25,000 contribution to get a seat at the table (DeLay subsequently met with the company). DeLay has joined the ranks of indicted Republicans, with three counts stemming from a money-laundering scheme funneling corporate donations to Texas legislative candidates (in a state that bans corporate donations for such purposes).

Despite such setbacks, the corporate cons have been the greatest beneficiaries of the Republican trifecta—the takeover of the White House, Congress, and the Supreme Court. A bankruptcy reform bill that eliminates bankruptcy protections, even for veterans and those suffering from catastrophic illnesses? Check. Tax-cuts for energy companies—with record-breaking profits—that have forestalled environmental safety increases? Check. A prescription-drug benefit that puts pharmaceutical industry profits ahead of sick Americans? Check.

These are boom times for the corporate cons.

Yet for a crowd that fetishizes its so-called business acumen, they have shown an inability to manage the nation's finances responsibly. Much to the disappointment of fiscal conservatives, the government has spent $2.3 trillion and had a $412 billion deficit in 2004 under the Bush administration, compared with the $1.8 trillion it spent and the $86 billion surplus it ran in the final year of the Clinton administration.[3]

THE THEOCONS

It was early 2005, and the nation was gripped by yet another cable-news-driven spectacle. Rather than a celebrity criminal trial or the latest missing pretty, single white female, this time the cameras focused on a feuding Florida family battling over the fate of Terri Schiavo, a brain-dead woman who had been in a coma for over a decade. Devoid of any hope of recovery, and acting on her previously stated wishes, her husband, Michael, sought to remove Terri from life-support systems. Terri's parents, under the grief-driven delusion that her condition was reversible, fought those efforts. Court after court ruled in favor of Michael Schiavo.

What was an ugly, private, and unfortunate family feud suddenly became fodder for Republican leaders looking to kowtow to religious fundamentalists who seek to legislate morality. A family crisis was quickly turned into a national one. Republicans everywhere tripped over themselves to rush to Terri Schiavo's parents' side, swearing fealty to their so-called "culture of life." MRIs showed that over half of Terri's brain was literally liquid mush and there was no hope of recovery, yet these people insisted that Terri's "life" somehow had to be saved.

Senate Majority Leader Bill Frist of Tennessee, a medical doctor, saw a few minutes of a heavily edited tape on TV and diagnosed that she was "not somebody in a persistent vegetative state." House Majority Leader Tom Delay, who had always smartly stayed out of the public limelight, used the incident to stage his national "coming out" party at the Family Research Council's theocon gathering.

The national cable news networks were all over the story, allowing right-wing surrogates to slander Michael Schiavo while running headlines like "The Fight to Save Terri." The Republicans and the Religious Right, led by James Dobson, Pat Robertson, and their huckster colleagues, claimed they were trying to "save a life," while Michael was trying to kill his wife.

As the Supreme Court rejected a final appeal from Terri's parents, Congress convened an emergency session while on recess, and Bush rushed to D.C. from one of his many vacations in Crawford, Texas, to sign a bill requiring Terri's life support to be maintained. (This was the same president who did not get back to work from another vacation in Crawford until three days after Hurricane Katrina wiped New Orleans and half the Gulf Coast off the map.) Democrats, predictably, were barely heard from.

And yet something amazing happened. Poll after opinion poll showed that between 80 and 90 percent of Americans sided with Terri's husband Michael, supporting his efforts to carry out her wish not to live in a vegetative state. Without a single prominent national political or media figure supporting Michael Schiavo's position, the American people had concluded that it wasn't the role of government, nor these self-appointed religious leaders, to tell people when and how they could die. In fact, legal groups reported a record number of downloads and inquiries about "living wills"—so people could insist on unplugging the life support if they were ever in Terri's situation.

Even though they are out of step with Americans, theocons hold a frightening sway over the Republican Party, increasingly calling the shots behind the facade of the party's "compassionate conservatism." Their numbers are huge—approximately twenty-six million voters in 2004 cited "moral issues" as their top concern, above terrorism, Iraq, or the economy. Bush won that crowd by a margin of 80 percent to 18 percent.[4] These are also the Republican shock troops, willing to get their hands dirty doing the hard work of politicking—the canvassing, phone banking, and get-out-the-vote efforts you would never catch a Wall Street type doing.

But there is a problem: These foot soldiers are a demanding bunch. They want *Roe v. Wade* overturned, they want emergency contraception banned, they want homosexuality criminalized, they want

Charles Darwin marginalized and creationism (and its newfangled disguise, "intelligent design") taught in science classes, and they want to proclaim from the rooftops that America is a Christian nation— *their* kind of Christian nation.

Theocons like Robertson and Dobson rail against the debased American culture, flooding the FCC with complaints of "indecency" on television and attempting to extend FCC reach into satellite radio and cable television. But their moral crusade only extends to issues of sex—premarital sex, homosexual sex, televised sex, presidential sex, adulterous sex, online sex. They see no moral issue involved in killing thousands of innocent Iraqi civilians, or as Pat Robertson publicly called for, in assassinating Hugo Chavez, the democratically elected president of Venezuela, because he threatened to cut off oil shipments to America. Assassination is not a moral question for such theocons, but oral sex among consenting adults or the fleeting flash of a singer's breast on TV—now that could lay the nation's soul to waste.

In 2004, Oklahoma sent one of the most fanatical of the Republican theocons, Tom Coburn, to the Senate. Coburn decried the Holocaust movie *Schindler's List* as "pornography" for the scene in which concentration camp Jews were herded naked into public showers. He claimed that girls in some Oklahoma high schools weren't allowed to go to the bathroom alone because of rampant lesbian sexual activity. He has urged the death penalty for doctors who perform abortions. His entire campaign against his Democratic opponent, Brad Carson, amounted to little more than "Carson loves gays and wants to kill babies." Recounting the campaign when we met him in Tulsa, Carson shook his head, trying to make sense of voters who responded to Coburn's message. "As the world around them becomes topsy-turvy, with the tumult of the economy, it makes people look for these kinds of age-old verities that they can root themselves in," Carson said. "The Right has been very successful in discrediting all of the theories of government that the Left had. On economic issues, people don't believe that the government can improve their lives much. Instead, people reach out to these kinds of fundamentalist notions and vote on lifestyle politics."

A large chunk of these theocons come from some of the most economically downtrodden groups in the nation, yet they end up believing that it's the Democrats who are a party of the elitists. That their beloved and morally upstanding Republican leaders never deliver the goods is irrelevant. "Here . . . is a rebellion against 'the establishment' that has wound up abolishing the tax on inherited estates," wrote Thomas Frank, in his book *What's the Matter with Kansas?* "Here is a movement whose response to the power structure is to make the rich even richer; whose answer to the inexorable degradation of working-class life is to lash out angrily at labor unions and liberal workplace-safety programs; whose solution to the rise of ignorance in America is to pull the rug out from under public education."

This seeming paradox—working-class theocons voting for a Republican party that cuts them off at the knees economically because it caters to its rich corporate sponsors—can be seen quite clearly in the 2004 election results. Of the twenty-eight states with the lowest per-capita income, Bush carried twenty-six. Republicans have convinced some of these poorest of the poor that government is powerless to improve their economic situation, so they focus on "values" issues instead: Terri Schiavo, abortion, gays, prayer in school, the Ten Commandments in public spaces. The promotion of these "values" becomes the government's top concern, even as the economy suffers and wars rage. The party that vowed to get the government off people's backs in the 1970s and 1980s has become the party that vows to get government into the classroom and the bedroom—everywhere but in the corporate boardroom.

Their numbers and zeal can't be discounted, and their role in pushing Bush over the top in 2004, while a grand victory of organizing, has also propelled this crowd to an influential place within the

GOP. Now they want payback. Instead, they get symbolic scraps—
plenty of lip service on issues of abortion and gay marriage, yet little
action. The Republicans can keep trotting out the same social issues
every election cycle and the theocons continue to turn out in droves.
"*Vote* to stop abortion; *receive* a rollback in capital gains taxes," writes
Frank. "*Vote* to screw those politically correct college professors;
receive electricity deregulation. . . . *Vote* to strike a blow against
elitism; *receive* a social order in which wealth is more concentrated
than ever before in our lifetimes, in which workers have been
stripped of power and CEOs are rewarded in a manner beyond imag-
ining." The louder the theocons push their agenda, the further away
from middle America they will continue to drift.

THE NEOCONS

A ninety-page white paper issued in September 2000 by an obscure
but well-connected think tank, the Project for the New American
Century (PNAC), laid out the precepts of the neoconservative
movement. Titled "Rebuilding America's Defenses," the authors
argued that modern threats to the United States could not be contained by diplomacy or détente, but had to be addressed by an aggressive, unilateralist foreign policy backed by a strong military. They
called for a new arms race in space, for bolstering the size of the
armed forces, and for the development of battlefield nuclear weapons.
The PNAC outlook was petulant, self-indulgent, severely myopic,
and extremely dangerous. If only its offices weren't occupied by the
likes of Donald Rumsfeld, Dick Cheney, Richard Perle, Paul
Wolfowitz, and Condoleezza Rice, and if only it were not heavily
funded by the Sarah Scaife Foundation, the John M. Olin
Foundation, and the Bradley Foundation, one might be tempted to
dismiss it out of hand.

It was in places like PNAC, far from the public eye and in a pseudo-intellectual realm, that these warmongers laid out their grand vision for American dominance of the world, especially of the Middle East. First among their targets was the so-called "low-hanging fruit"—Saddam's weakened Iraq. With Iraq's security forces severely damaged by the 1991 Gulf War and a decade of sanctions, these neocons thought invading Iraq would provide the perfect lesson to the world—submit to the lone remaining superpower or suffer American "shock and awe." And after devising fantastic theories with no basis in reality (for instance, that invading U.S. forces would be greeted as liberators), they sent good men and women to their deaths with hardly a twinge of conscience. Bush's "doctrine of preemption" was a triumph of these war-happy elites who thought they could sit in their gilded offices and remake the world by moving armies around their game of Risk.

Neocons don't suffer critics gladly, as even mere questioning of their infallibility and wisdom will jumpstart their considerable smear machine. Valerie Plame was a covert CIA operative working on weapons of mass destruction issues when the agency asked her husband, Joe Wilson, a former ambassador to Gabon in Africa, to investigate charges that Iraq had attempted to purchase yellowcake uranium from Niger. Wilson investigated the charges and, convinced there was nothing to them, reported back to the CIA, which concurred with his findings. Yet somehow, the charge that "Saddam Hussein recently sought significant quantities of uranium from Africa" made it into George Bush's 2003 State of the Union address as he whipped up war fever as a prelude to the invasion of Iraq. Wilson, aghast at the false claims, finally went public on July 6, 2003, with an op-ed piece in the *New York Times*.

Unable to deal with this relatively mild public rebuke, the Bush administration lashed out at Wilson, capping its attack with leaks of his wife's secret identity to a series of journalists. Conservative columnist

Robert Novak went public with Plame's identity on July 14, 2003. The ensuing revelations and the investigations by special counsel Patrick J. Fitzgerald resulted in the indictment in October 2005 of Cheney's chief of staff, Lewis "Scooter" Libby; jail time for Judith Miller, a reporter for the *New York Times*; and the continued investigation of Bush's right-hand man, Karl Rove. Yet while a CIA agent was outed, endangering her work on nuclear proliferation and the network of companies and other intelligence assets (including people) she used in her undercover role, the administration chose to close ranks and protect its own rather than punish them for a serious breach of national security.

What the Plame affair revealed was the ugly underbelly of the neocons in the Bush administration, especially their "you're with us or against us" approach to foreign policy—and apparently toward domestic critics as well.

Unfortunately for the neocons (and the world), none of their grand designs are producing favorable results. The number of terrorist attacks in 2004 broke records, a fact sheepishly admitted to by the U.S. State Department after its first draft of a report on terrorism falsely claimed dramatic declines in the number of such attacks. The Taliban is resurgent in Afghanistan and, on any given day, controls one or more of that nation's provinces. And, of course, Osama bin Laden and company operate in and out of the Pakistan/Afghanistan border with near impunity.

The Iraq War, the biggest "achievement" of the neocons, has turned out to be an abject and tragic failure. It was always an easy invasion, given our nation's superior military, but never a winnable war, given the cost of occupation. All the incessant talk of "weapons of mass destruction" amounted to a pile of lies. They claimed the war would pay for itself from Iraqi oil revenues; instead, the war has already cost the United States $250 billion. And the promise of cheap gasoline has been shattered with $3-per-gallon gas. They predicted that invading U.S. forces would be showered with flower petals; instead they've been showered with bullets, mortars, shrapnel, and car bombs. They promised that the new Iraqi government would be a stable and prosperous pro-Israel model democracy, a beacon of hope amid an autocratic Middle East; instead, it is turning out to be a theocratic regime that may end up with a long-running civil war between its dominant ethnic groups.

And then there is the death and dying. More than 2,000 American men and women have been killed, while estimates of Iraqi dead range from 25,000 by the United Nations Development Program to 100,000 by the *Lancet*, the British medical journal. No one weeps over Saddam Hussein's ouster. Good riddance. But was his ouster worth billions of dollars and tens of thousands of deaths? Was it worth handing Iran a friendly regime on its western border? Was it worth sapping our military readiness and ability to respond to genuine threats? Was it worth taking our eyes off Afghanistan and Osama bin Laden?

Yet after this string of stunning defeats, none of Bush's neocon allies have been discredited or tarred and feathered.

Deputy Secretary of Defense Paul Wolfowitz was rewarded with a plum assignment as president of the World Bank. Secretary of Defense Donald Rumsfeld was asked to stay on at the Pentagon for Bush's second term. National Security Advisor Condoleezza Rice was promoted to secretary of state. The neocon spy at Colin Powell's State Department, John Bolton, was rewarded with the U.N. ambassadorship (a recess appointment that even several Senate Republicans did not support).

The irony, of course, is that their initiatives have made the United States less safe by inflaming anti-American sentiment worldwide, filling the ranks of terrorist groups, and diverting resources into expensive foreign entanglements rather than homeland security (vividly proven by the chaotic, incompetent federal response to Hurricane Katrina).

But keeping people in fear while engaging in the so-called war on terror paid wonderful political dividends for Bush and the Republicans in both 2002 and 2004, elections in which terrorism and Iraq trumped Democratic advantages in virtually every domestic issue. It's a tactic they hope to repeat in future elections, no matter how much it might hurt the nation.

THE PALEOCONS

Once a dominant segment of the Republican coalition, the old-world conservatives and libertarians are now at odds with the direction of the Republican Party. These paleocons are instinctively xenophobic and anti-immigrant, hostile to foreign interventions and "nation-building," and paranoid on border-security issues. They cling to the English-only 1950s and an increasingly non-Republican philosophy of smaller government and protection of individual liberties.

The split between the neocons and the paleocons during the run-up to the Iraq War showed just how far the once powerful paleocon forces of the Republican Party had fallen. Hostile to government power, paleocons only demanded that the state triumph over communism because it threatened their worship of individualism. Paleocons like Pat Buchanan and Robert Novak were the original small-government conservatives, abhorring Franklin D. Roosevelt's New Deal and wanting to abolish welfare.

Absent a foreign foe since the demise of communism, paleocons have lately been obsessed with more homegrown "enemies": immigrants from south of the border who threaten to turn this nation into "MexAmerica," as Buchanan put it. "[W]e are being invaded, and the president of the United States is not doing his duty to protect the states against that invasion," wrote Buchanan in an August 2005 syndicated column. "Some courageous Republican, to get the attention of this White House, should drop into the hopper a bill of impeachment, charging George W. Bush with a conscious refusal to uphold his oath and defend the states of the Union against 'invasion.'"[5]

The paleos see the corporate cons encourage undocumented immigration to drive down wages, they see the theocons trample over privacy rights, and they see the neocons engage in expensive foreign entanglements, yet they are powerless to do anything about it. They are a dying breed, left behind by a party in thrall to the corporatists who wield the power, the theocons who deliver the electoral ground troops, and the neocons who infest the halls of the Pentagon, the State Department, and White House.

Libertarians in the Republican Party are in no better shape. Once upon a time, the Republican ideology called for reducing the size of the government and protecting personal liberties. As such, it was the natural home for those who distrusted government and wanted to see its influence diminished. The fact that Republicans still hold on to these voters despite the massive growth of government under their watch and the assault on personal liberties through vehicles like the Patriot Act is further testament to the party's coalition-building efforts.

The Second Amendment pro-gun crowd, an offshoot of the libertarian faction, is one of the few single-issue constituency groups inside the Republican Party, and the National Rifle Association is perhaps the most powerful issue group in the country. There was a time when the Republican Party was their home, as Democrats worked hard to enact gun-control legislation. But that battle is over, and except for skirmishes in urban jurisdictions, gun control is essentially dead inside the Democratic Party and certainly dead at the federal level. That major shift will take a few years to filter down to voters throughout the country, but it should further weaken the Republican hold on gun owners.

So what we have when we look at the twenty-first-century conservative movement is a rather fragile coalition under the umbrella of the Republican Party: the corporate cons are a single-issue group looking out for deregulation, tax cuts, and subsidies; the theocons are obsessed with gays and abortion and prayer in public places; the neocons played their trump card in Iraq and are losing their hand; and the paleocons have been mostly marginalized in their anti-immigrant, isolationist corner.

Not one of the dominant Republican groups above knows how to—or even cares to—run a government that manages money well while providing basic public services. And at no time before was that salient fact made clearer until a historic hurricane hit the Gulf Coast in late August 2005.

THE KATRINA TRAGEDY

The week didn't begin well for Bush or his Republican brethren. On the tail end of his five-week vacation in Crawford, Bush whined about antiwar protesters led by Cindy Sheehan, camped out near his faux ranch, disturbing his efforts to "get on with his life." Sheehan had lost her son to Bush's Iraq adventure, and her impromptu vigil in the Texas heat was generating favorable press and attention. With his "compassion" reservoirs already running low, Bush was about to see the last few days of his five-week vacation go from "bad" to "disastrous." Moving up through the Gulf of Mexico, Hurricane Katrina was gaining steam. At Category 5 and with sustained winds of over 160 miles per hour, Katrina was about to turn Bush's presidency upside down.

On Sunday, August 28, 2005, the National Weather Service issued a bulletin that warned of the dire situation awaiting the region upon the hurricane's landfall, saying people risked death if they stayed in the hurricane's path. Unfortunately, a significant portion of New Orleans' mostly African American underclass was trapped. Levees around New Orleans that had been underfunded by years of budget cuts gave way. The resulting floods submerged large parts of the city. Entire swaths of Louisiana, Mississippi, and Alabama were destroyed.

Meanwhile, Bush spent his time vacationing, eating birthday cake with John McCain in Arizona on August 29, playing guitar with country star Mark Willis in San Diego the next day, and giving speeches about Iraq, World War II, and the dismantling of Social Security. The man who had rushed with a few hours notice to D.C. in the dead of the night to sign the Terri Schiavo bill had to be dragged from his vacation to D.C. three days after Katrina hit. While the Gulf Coast was a helicopter ride away from his Crawford hideout, Bush decided to "survey" the damage from a mile up from Air Force One. Pictures of Bush pathetically looking out the window at the damage were a political disaster—he looked weak, ineffective, and aloof, all at once. When he finally "took action" (after his poll numbers started plummeting), his inability to connect with the pain of regular folk was tragically comic. In his first visit to the region, Bush was torn up—about Trent Lott's beachside vacation home. "We've got a lot of rebuilding to do. . . . The good news is—and it's hard for some to see it now—that out of this chaos is going to come a fantastic Gulf Coast, like it was before. Out of the rubbles of Trent Lott's house—he's lost his entire house— there's going to be a fantastic house. And I'm looking forward to sitting on the porch. [Laughter]"[6] At a stop in New Orleans, Bush joked about his party days in the French Quarter while people were still dying from the lack of government response.

Michael Chertoff, secretary of the Department of Homeland Security, seemed to be clueless about what was happening on the ground, telling a National Public Radio reporter that he wasn't aware that thousands of people were stranded in the Convention Center in

New Orleans even though TV stations had reported from the scene. And of course, there was Mr. Incompetent himself, Michael "Brownie, you're doing a heck of a job!" Brown, the head of FEMA, who tried to lay all the blame for the incredibly slow federal response on local and state officials (especially the Democrats, like Louisiana governor Kathleen Blanco). Meanwhile, e-mails subsequently released showed that Brown had been more concerned with his attire, bragging after a television appearance about his outfit from Nordstrom, "I am a fashion god."[7] Responding to an e-mail from Marty Bahamonde, a FEMA worker in New Orleans, who told him "the situation is past critical" and people were near death, Brown's entire response was, "Thanks for the update. Anything specific I need to do or tweak?"

The nation got another chance to see those "compassionate conservatives" in action when thousands of people were evacuated from the Gulf Coast and sent to the Astrodome in Houston. The president's mother and former first lady Barbara Bush visited the evacuees—and seemed amused. "What I'm hearing, which is sort of scary, is that they all want to stay in Texas. Everybody is so overwhelmed by the hospitality. And so many of the people in the arena here, you know, were underprivileged anyway so this [chuckle]—this is working very well for them."[8] House Majority Leader Tom DeLay cornered a couple of bewildered kids stranded in the Astrodome. "Now tell me the truth boys, is this kind of fun?"[9]

Meanwhile, House Speaker Dennis Hastert, a Republican from Illinois, suggested publicly that perhaps New Orleans needed to be bulldozed. Republican senator Rick Santorum of Pennsylvania seemed more concerned with finding fault with hurricane victims than with ensuring federal help was provided, urging penalties for those too poor to leave New Orleans and who had lost everything. "I mean, you have people who don't heed those warnings and then put people at risk as a result of not heeding those warnings," Santorum said in an interview with a Pittsburgh TV station. "There may be a need to look at tougher penalties on those who decide to ride it out and understand that there are consequences to not leaving." Antitax crusaders sifted through death records to see if any Katrina-related deaths could be used to advance their efforts to repeal the estate tax.[10] And of course, Joe Allbaugh was busy hustling post-hurricane reconstruction business for Halliburton.

Right on cue, the definition of theocon "compassion" became readily apparent. The overwhelming majority of Christians surely felt compassion for those suffering in the wake of Katrina, but the fundamentalists seeking an American theocracy couldn't resist assigning blame. "God judged New Orleans for the sin of shedding innocent blood through abortion," said Steve Lefeminc of South Carolina's Columbia Christians for Life. And Michael Marcavage of Philadelphia, who runs the evangelistic organization Repent America, noted that a gay-and-lesbian street festival had been scheduled in New Orleans when Katrina hit: "The day Bourbon Street and the French Quarter was flooded was the day that 125,000 homosexuals were going to be celebrating sin in the streets. . . . We're calling it an act of God."[11]

Blaming Katrina on gays was pretty extreme, but well within character for the theocons. And it wasn't just fringe outfits either. "After September 11, 2001, 'God bless America' was on everyone's lips. But what, exactly, are we asking God to bless—a nation moving at breakneck speed toward homosexual marriage, a nation awash in pornography, a nation in which our children are indoctrinated in perversion in the public schools, a nation in which most public displays of the Ten Commandments are considered offensive to the Constitution, a nation in which the elite does all in its considerable power to efface our Biblical heritage?" asked the Reverend Rick Scarborough of Vision America as he began his Katrina analysis in his newsletter.[12] The group's 2006 conference (titled "The War on Christians and the

Values Voter in 2006") included speeches by Senator Sam
Brownback of Kansas (considered a serious Republican presidential
candidate for 2008) and Representative Tom DeLay (house majority
leader until his indictment in Texas). "We are sowing the wind,"
Scarborough wrote. "Surely, we shall reap the whirlwind. One other
factor which must be considered: Days before Katrina nearly wiped
New Orleans off the map, 9,000 Jewish residents of Gaza were driven
from their homes with the full support of the United States government. Could this be a playing out of prophesy [sic] ('I will bless that
nation that blesses you, and curse the nation that curses you')?"

For their part, the neocons had played their own role in the disaster—
by diverting the National Guard resources to Iraq and Afghanistan.
When Katrina hit, the Guard had only half its usual equipment—
helicopters, trucks, and Humvees—available because the rest was
diverted to fight the "war on terror," the *Boston Globe* reported on
September 2, 2005. Meanwhile, in Louisiana and Mississippi, the
hardest hit states, about 40 percent of the National Guard was in
Iraq, the newspaper reported. And suddenly, a Republican political
establishment unconcerned with the hundreds of billions poured into
faraway Iraq became agitated at the thought of spending the tens of
billions necessary to rebuild one of America's own cities.

We have two competing worldviews in American politics. One says
that public spending is a disease that does more harm than good and
that government is best kept small. The other says that government
can be a force for good and can help make people's lives better.

During the week following the hurricane, with New Orleans turned
into Lake George, we saw the tragic consequences of the Republican
"small government" philosophy. There were two obvious disasters
that week—the hurricane itself, which was an unavoidable act of
nature, and the lack of government leadership and response to the
hurricane's aftermath, which was avoidable.

But there was also a third disaster—the conservative worldview itself, crashing and burning as ideology met reality. Grover Norquist is the central figure of the Vast Right-Wing Conspiracy (VRWC), coordinating efforts among the Right's allied organizations and funneling money to them. While his day job is head of Americans for Tax Reform, his influence goes far beyond his organization. Norquist has never been shy about his goal, having famously said once that "I don't want to abolish government. I simply want to reduce it to the size where I can drag it into the bathroom and drown it in the bathtub." Bush has been a dues-paying member of the Norquist fan club, and his tax policies have been straight out of the Norquist playbook—reduce and abolish as many taxes as possible (Norquist famously compared the estate tax to the Holocaust). From that antigovernment perspective, running up deficits is not necessarily a bad thing, because it forces government to be cut down to the bone.

Yet in New Orleans, as the city lay in ruins and underwater, that bathtub quote suddenly seemed disturbingly apropos of the dominant Republican worldview. Katrina flooded New Orleans because the canals and levees were not properly funded by the Bush administration, and people's suffering was greatly exacerbated by the incredibly slow government response. Republicans showed their compassion by blaming the victims, blaming gays, threatening to bulldoze what was left of New Orleans, and by cracking inappropriate jokes.

In the end, we had more than 1,300 Americans dead and more than $100 billion in property damage. It was a stark reminder that the Republican Party is clueless when it comes to the basic task of governing and meeting the needs of its citizens. But the Republicans didn't get to be the dominant political force in D.C. overnight. What we see today is the culmination of four decades of sustained work by the conservative movement. It is also an indictment of the Democratic establishment that never saw it coming.

HOW DID WE GET HERE?

A flight from Ronald Reagan Washington National Airport in D.C. to George Bush Intercontinental Airport in Houston is not the sort of thing that makes liberals walk with pep in their step. Who needs more reminders of Republican successes over the past two decades? It wasn't that long ago that this very same flight would have been from Washington National to Houston Intercontinental. Those airports weren't afflicted with their current monikers until the late 1990s. To the GOP victors go the spoils.

But we weren't in Texas to ponder airport names—or for a vacation in Crawford. Rather, we set out to find the Texas Democratic Party, or more accurately, to find out what the heck happened to it. Because Texas was a little different from the rest of the South—a reliably and solidly Democratic state lost to the Republicans in a few short election cycles. As the fortunes of southern Democrats waned, so did the fortunes of Democrats nationally. And as the fortunes of Texas Republicans rose—well, we know which state dominates the D.C. power structure at the moment.

Forty years ago, Texas also dominated the D.C. power structure, but those politicians were a different kind of Texan—they were Democrats, like Lyndon B. Johnson. The "good old days," in terms of the Democratic Party, lasted from roughly the 1930s into the 1960s. It was an era of strong majorities, seven of nine presidential election wins, and a healthy working-class coalition that supported the development of a liberal society. The New Deal had brought the nation out of the Great Depression by reforming the U.S. economy, strengthening labor unions, employing millions of unemployed Americans in public works projects, creating Social Security, and generally proving that government can be a force for good. It was the crowning achievement for the Democratic Party and a seminal accomplishment for the United States in the twentieth century.

Even Republican presidents governed liberally. Dwight D. Eisenhower, rather than scale back the fruits of the New Deal, *expanded* them, creating the Department of Health, Education, and Welfare, building the federal interstate system, and expanding Social Security. Government was ascendant, embraced by the public, media, and pundit class, and both the Republican and Democratic establishments. And it paid huge dividends to the Democratic Party for decades.

By the 1960s, it brought together a coalition of immigrants, farmers, and workers through policies that generated economic stability, security, and increased standards of living, while weakening corporate dominance of government. And the government's agenda was the people's agenda—civil and voting rights, the war on poverty, new environmental regulations, and increased educational opportunities. After the landslide victory by Texan Lyndon B. Johnson over conservative Republican Barry Goldwater in the 1964 presidential election (Goldwater opposed both the Civil Rights and Voting Rights Acts), the economic and social well-being of Americans mirrored the success of the Democratic majority. The new president, LBJ, waxed poetic that as a young boy, "I first learned that the government is not an enemy of the people. It *is* the people."

Those weren't just the good old days, they were the *glory* days. Respected presidential scholar James MacGregor Burns wrote at the time, "By every test we have, this is as surely a liberal epoch as the late 19th Century was a conservative one."

Somewhere though, between the mid sixties and early seventies, liberals lost their way and have still not recovered. Historians and political scientists can argue over how the backlash began: whether it was a bad economy or corporate hostility toward expanded governmental services, or the northeastern/southern divide over race and civil rights, or the emergence of the religious right and its cultural war against social progressives. What's obvious is that in the 1960s and 1970s, while the

Democrat's New Deal coalition was collapsing, a very cohesive—and very conservative—political movement was emerging.

Just four years after the Goldwater disaster, Republicans came together in 1968 and elected Richard Nixon as president. Sometimes, doing the right thing trumps all calculations, and surrendering the South to the Republicans in exchange for Civil Rights was a trade worth making, even if it cost votes. LBJ understood the electoral ramifications, telling a presidential aide just after passage of the Civil Rights Act, "There goes the South for a generation." Republicans were too unscrupulous to let this opportunity slip away. Nixon planned and executed the infamous "southern strategy" (demonize blacks in the South to get the white, blue-collar rural vote) to explicitly embrace those opposed to civil rights. Nixon rode that bigotry in the South to the White House in 1968 and 1972. And Republicans pressed their advantage on other social issues, painting the Democrats as the party of "Amnesty, Acid, and Abortion." Nixon had legitimate conservative credentials and a killer political instinct that eventually led to his downfall, but his governing style still reflected the liberalism of the times. It was Nixon who created the Environmental Protection Agency, the Office of Minority Business Enterprise, and the Supplemental Security Income program. He established détente with China and negotiated reductions in nuclear arms with the Soviet Union. He got the space shuttle program off the ground.

But behind the scenes, down in the trenches, movement conservatives were plotting and executing the takeover of local parties, enacting a bottom-up purge of moderate and liberal Republicans, and promoting Goldwater-style conservatism. Goldwater may have lost his election, but his ideas were powering a vast new nationwide movement against the dominant establishment elite.

Lewis Powell, just a few months shy of joining the Supreme Court in 1971, penned a memo to a friend at the U.S. Chamber of Commerce that encapsulated the growing momentum toward a broad-based conservative movement. "Survival of what we call the free enterprise system, lies in organization, in careful long-range planning and implementation, in consistency of action over an indefinite period of years, in the scale of financing available only through joint effort, and in the political power available only through united action and national organizations," he wrote. Those words eventually helped fuel nascent efforts to create the most sophisticated, well-funded political propaganda machine in world history to combat "communists, New Leftists, and other revolutionaries that would destroy the entire system, both political and economic."

Rob Stein, a former Clinton administration official and venture capitalist, created quite a stir in 2004 with his famed PowerPoint presentation entitled "The Conservative Message Machine's Money Matrix," which documented how the conservative movement—and a handful of its wealthy benefactors—set out in the 1970s to build a vast network of think tanks, training groups, media outlets, and policy centers that now constitute an effective infrastructure to promote the conservative agenda. (We'll hear more from Stein in the fourth chapter.)

The effort was financed by hundreds of millions of dollars from six wealthy families—Richard Mellon Scaife in Pittsburgh, Harry Bradley in Milwaukee, John Olin in New York City, the Richardson family in North Carolina, Joseph Coors in Denver, and David and Charles Koch in Wichita. Together, their foundations had assets of over $1.7 billion and the strategic vision to funnel their resources into this new ideological machine.

In many ways, the political epicenter of this conservative movement was the South, and Texas in particular was breeding some of the movement's brightest stars. The shift was startling. Going back to the days of Reconstruction, Texas, like most southern states, had its own version of a two-party system—liberal Democrats and conservative Democrats. However, in 1978, Bill Clements Jr. became the first

Republican governor of Texas in over 100 years. Everybody thought it was a fluke, and that sentiment seemed justified when Democrat Mark White beat him four years later in 1982, and Democrats swept every single statewide elected office. They were back on top. It was at this time, however, that a new player arrived on the Texas political scene. Direct-mail guru Karl Rove put a bull's-eye on the state's top Democrats and set out to take each one down—with an unconventional strategy. Rove went for the jugular—cutting off big business money flowing to Democrats—by getting Republicans elected to the Texas judiciary. As these judges handed down pro-business rulings, those businesses responded by shifting their campaign contribution dollars to Republicans.

"A lesser consultant or analyst might have overlooked that. They might have said, 'You know what? I'm going to go and get some people to run for the legislature.' And 'I'm going to get some people to run for county office,'" Jim Moore, author of *Bush's Brain* (a.k.a. Karl Rove), told us when we met over lunch at an eatery in Austin. "But, what Karl has always been better at than anybody else is his long vision. This guy can see eight moves down the chessboard, over the horizon, beyond the event horizon. He creates environments. They're not environments where he's always in complete control, but they are environments ultimately favorable to Republican candidates."

Over in Washington, Ronald Reagan's 1980 election marked the first time this new conservative movement gained a foothold in the federal government. By that time, Republicans had learned to make the "southern strategy" more explicit. Reagan, in fact, announced his 1980 campaign for president in Neshoba County, Mississippi—the place where the Ku Klux Klan murdered three civil rights workers in 1964 (depicted in the movie *Mississippi Burning*). All across the South, white southerners were becoming Republicans.

Longtime Democratic consultant George Strong worked the trenches in Texas during this era and was witness to mass defections from the Democratic Party to the Republicans. "It suddenly became okay for businessmen and professionals to vote Republican because all their neighbors were doing it, everybody at the country club was doing it, people in the law firm were doing it," he told us at his hurricane-proof home in Galveston. "There really was no reason to stay Democrat because what did you have to do? You had to defend that we were the party of only minorities and gays and women's-libbers and so forth."

While Democrat Ann Richards won the governor's mansion in 1990, she was essentially the last gasp of the state's Democratic establishment. She was swept aside in 1994 by George W. Bush, under the skillful management of Karl Rove. The Rove-led Republican takeover of Texas was complete. That same year, while Newt Gingrich and his Contract with America helped Republicans take Congress and battle Bill Clinton in D.C., Rove set the stage to export his handiwork to the national arena.

Would it be a stretch to credit or blame Texas for what we see today at the national level? "I don't think it's a stretch," Moore tells us. "I think there were certain political forces driving Republican gains around the country that would not have come together without Karl acting as a catalyst. Karl knew that this was the future and was setting up an infrastructure that has now grown and sent tentacles out all across the country."

The Republican Congress wasn't able to make much progress with its agenda while Clinton was in office. But that all changed in 2000. Despite eight years of peace, prosperity, budget surpluses, and myriad legislative accomplishments, Al Gore, the Democratic nominee, wasn't able to hold on to the White House. A hostile media and a mature and rabid right-wing noise machine plagued Gore, contributing to his defeat. But also devastating was the new and improved Republican brand, courtesy of George W. Bush and his frighteningly effective brain trust. The sea change was complete.

The Republican right wing has been able to hijack this country because the Democratic establishment hasn't worked to stop them. Democrats ignored the threatening clouds and sat idly as Republicans notched their electoral wins.

Despite eight prosperous years under Clinton, the fact remains that it's been a while since Democrats garnered a simple majority presidential vote. Clinton didn't win 50 percent of the popular vote in either of his two elections in 1992 and 1996. In fact, we need to go back to 1976 for the last time a Democrat won more than 50 percent of the popular vote in a presidential election, and back to 1964 for when a Democrat last won more than a narrow 50.1 percent of that vote.

And here's the rub: Despite forty years of trying to gain a majority and failing, there are few indications that the Democratic establishment is even rethinking its ways. The predominant view seems to be that we just need to raise more money, buy more television airtime, prove we are not afraid of waging wars abroad, and wait for the Republicans to self-destruct.

The Democrats' New Deal coalition is long dead. It's not coming back. Neither will Democrats ever replace the Republicans by trying to move to the center and becoming the party of business interests. Democrats have to stand for something different, providing a stark alternative to the pro-corporatist, antigovernment agenda of the Republican Party. The Democratic Party, which was clearly identified from the 1930s to the 1960s with improving the economic status of *all* Americans, is now effectively portrayed as more concerned with social issues and "special interests," including abortion rights, gay and lesbian rights, gun control, environmental regulation, labor unions, and trial lawyers.

Not long after the 2004 election, as Republicans drunk with power counted their victories, House Majority Leader Tom DeLay of Texas took stock of the situation. "The Republican Party is a permanent majority for the future of this country," DeLay said. "We're going to be able to lead this country in the direction we've been dreaming of for years." In early 2005, at a party retreat, he offered a sequel. "If 1994 was the year we stopped thinking like a permanent minority, 2004 is the year we start thinking like a permanent majority: unified, aggressive, rightfully confident of victory."

BACKLASH INSURANCE

Despite DeLay's blathering about a "permanent majority," there is little confidence among conservative circles that they can maintain their current level of electoral dominance for the long term. They know they won't be able to count on winning elections perpetually given the cyclical nature of politics—a realization no doubt reinforced by their woeful governing performance and the scandals and legal troubles besetting their party. So they are working to rig the system to ensure as many advantages as they can gain—controlling voting machines, gerrymandering congressional districts, targeting Democratic donors, suppressing Democratic-leaning voters, and packing the courts with conservative ideologues. They have implemented "backlash insurance" to protect them and their excesses against the will of the majority.

The most far-reaching strategy may be the effort to remake the judiciary—the same strategy Rove pursued in Texas in the 1980s.

"What I fear most is that in the last twenty or thirty years, right-wing Republicans have had a grand vision, and if their grand vision comes true—and they're *this close* to having it come true—it would dramatically alter for decades the structure of the American government, the functions of the American government and how the Constitution is interpreted," Ralph Neas, president of People for the American Way, told us at his office in Washington, D.C. "I'm talking about the real conservative thinkers who want, not necessarily a permanent Republican majority, but an America that reflects for decades the values of the right wing of the Republican Party."

In other words, it's less important to be a majority party in Congress or control the White House or state governments than it is to have a society that has been reengineered to reflect conservative dogma. The longer Republicans can forestall their inevitable fall from grace and power, and the more judges they can place in the judiciary, the closer they come to that realignment of American society. While legislators mark their terms in two, four, or six years, and while presidents come and go every four or eight years, federal judges are appointed for life. The grand conservative vision includes an overhaul of the Constitution, and to do that, the holders of this vision need to place relatively young conservative judges on the bench, ensuring that long after voters finally oust the Republicans, their political interpretations of the Constitution continue to impede progress.

Neas recounted an exchange he had with Ralph Nader over the dangers of a Republican takeover of the judiciary: "Nader said, 'If you're right, there'll be a revolution in this country. Take away *Roe v. Wade*, take away this, take away that.' I said, 'I understand this theory. I understand that if you get enough people mad, they're going to throw the Republican Party out of power. But the way the Republicans are doing it, it won't matter if they're out of power as long as they make sure that we don't have the money and the law is on their side by a five-four, six-three majority for twenty or thirty years.' It's a great strategy."

There are other strategies as well. In *Off Center*, authors Jacob Hacker and Paul Pierson (who coined the term "backlash insurance") note that Republicans have used the machinery of government to pass reactionary legislation but formulate it in ways that mask the true costs. Bush's tax cuts contained "sunset" provisions that allowed the administration to claim a lower price tag and a smaller effect on the national debt than would be the case if they were permanent. Bush, of course, had no intention of letting the tax cuts expire. When the pain hits, the laws in question will be too entrenched to easily revoke, or else Democrats, finally in charge, will take this hit for fixing the problems by raising taxes or cutting spending.

Republicans are also taking aim at the Democratic Party's major funders, much as Rove did in Texas in the 1980s. Lately, that would mean targeting labor unions and trial lawyers. For example, a ballot measure in the November 2005 California elections, backed by Governor Arnold Schwarzenegger, sought to prevent unions from using dues for political purposes unless approved by individual union members. Union busting and antiunion initiatives have the dual effect of freeing corporations from an organized labor force while simultaneously drying up union funds for political work. The measure was defeated 54 to 46 percent by voters. But it wasn't a total failure from the Republican standpoint—unions had to spend $43 million to defeat it.[13]

Trial lawyers, one of the largest sources of funding for the Democratic Party and its candidates, are under fierce attack by the current administration and Congress. Bush and the Republican Party have heavily pushed "tort reform" legislation, which includes such measures as a federal cap on damage awards for medical malpractice, forcing class-action cases into federal courts, and creating a national settlement of outstanding asbestos-related cases. These measures have a dual purpose: to keep some major Republican constituents (doctors, large corporations) happy and to slash the money earned by plaintiffs' attorneys, and consequently, the Democratic Party. Largely in reaction to this intimidation, some trial lawyers and labor groups have begun contributing to Republicans.

But perhaps the most effective strategy to ensure an ongoing

Republican advantage in future years has been to tinker with the machinery of voting and the administration of elections. Republicans gerrymander congressional districts whenever possible, not just at the end of each decade as has been tradition, but midterm whenever local politics allow it (that is, through Republican takeovers of state governments). In recent years, Republicans successfully pulled off mid-decade redistricting in Texas and in Georgia. They were able to turn probable congressional losses in 2004 into a gain of three seats because they gerrymandered five additional seats in Texas. Another effort in Colorado failed because of judicial intervention.

Democrats, despite controlling the redistricting apparatus in several states like New Mexico, Louisiana, and Illinois, where additional seats could easily be redrawn, have failed to follow suit. Such indifference by Democrats in the face of the determined, relentless conservative machine is quite common.

Rigging the electoral system to their advantage also includes ballot-box issues—creating institutional roadblocks for Democratic-leaning voters. While Diebold (and other electronic) voting machines that lack a paper trail have garnered lots of the attention and controversy, most voter suppression efforts are far less sexy while being quite effective. As Democratic Congressman John Conyers of Michigan noted in his landmark report on the 2004 mess in Ohio,[14] voters in Cleveland's inner city had to endure eight-hour-long voting lines, while suburban voters got in and out in fifteen minutes. On December 15, 2004, the *Washington Post* reported that in Franklin County, "27 of the 30 wards with the most machines per registered voter showed majorities for Bush. At the other end of the spectrum, six of the seven wards with the fewest machines delivered large margins for Kerry."

Ohio's Republican secretary of state disenfranchised hundreds, probably thousands of predominantly minority and Democratic voters by restricting provisional ballots and failing to mail out absentee ballots in time. The Ohio Republican Party selectively targeted 35,000 predominantly minority voters for intimidation and vote suppression, in direct violation of existing legal consent decrees barring such behavior. They used voter challenges in Democratic and minority districts to slow down the pace of voting, disenfranchising thousands discouraged by the long lines. Mark Weaver, a lawyer for the Ohio Republican Party, was quoted in Conyers' report, admitting the challenges "can't help but create chaos, longer lines and frustration."

Maybe Bush had the votes to win Ohio cleanly, but there's no doubt the Republican machinery was working hard just in case—to steal the election as it had in Florida in 2000. Given how close the electoral balance was in places like Ohio, if you can add up enough suppression efforts to give you an additional 1 to 2 percent of the vote, it could be enough to defy the will of the electorate.

NO TIME TO LOSE

Perhaps nothing is fueling the rise of a new progressive movement more than the lack of urgency from the Democratic political establishment in D.C. Twelve years after Newt Gingrich and his Contract with America helped sweep Democrats into a political Siberia, the Democratic Party and its coalition of single-issue groups and its consultant class continue to act as if the party still holds a majority. There is no move underway to rethink and develop a core set of governing principles to persuade the American public. Progressive-issue groups—pro-choice, environmental, civil rights, minorities—continue to operate much as they have for the past several decades, apparently undeterred by their repeated failures, refusing to acknowledge the changing media and political landscape that has made many of their efforts, at best, ineffective or obsolete, and at worse, counterproductive.

So here we are with the harsh reality of a Republican Party run amok, a midterm election looming, and a Democratic Party that's ill-prepared to win elections. If progressives want to win now, it is up to the new people-powered movement to get active. But first, we must take an unflinching look at our own party to understand where we went wrong and how we might fix it.

THIS AIN'T NO PARTY

"The Democratic Party for too long has been a group of constituencies instead of a party."
—Howard Dean, speaking in Helena, Montana, June 4, 2005

The Democratic Party stands for everything, yet stands for nothing. It's a gaggle of special and narrow interests, often in conflict with each other, rarely working in concert to advance their common causes. Members of each issue group—environmentalists, pro-choice activists, civil libertarians, plaintiffs' attorneys, and so on—promote their agenda above all others and show little or no understanding of the larger progressive values they share with the other groups. And so the whole is never really greater than the sum of its parts.

Progressive groups share many of the same limited funding sources, and are in constant competition with each other for the same precious donor dollars. Deborah and Andy Rappaport of Silicon Valley are major Democratic donors and have seen this first-hand. "The assumption among the issue groups is that there is a finite pool of money, and it comes from a finite list of people," says Deborah Rappaport. "Everybody has the same list. Everybody is trying to scream louder, or give away more free shrimp, or do whatever it is that gets their message heard, to get their remit envelopes sent back first."

The conservative movement, on the other hand, has a massive funding machine ensuring that its advocacy groups are flush with cash. While ours struggle on a daily basis to keep their operations running, the conservatives receive multiyear funding commitments and have enough money to wine and dine politicians at snazzy restaurants. Their groups can focus most of their energy on their issues; our groups spend way too much time fundraising.

And when they're not fundraising, they're doing the research, lobbying politicians, chasing media coverage, monitoring their opponents, and busily working in their silos. Just as they have been since the 1960s, Democrats act as though they are still in power in D.C. and just need to tweak their talking points and dispatch their lobbyists to Capitol Hill to get their legislation through. The world has changed, conservatives are running the show, and yet these groups don't seem to grasp the need for working hand in hand with other progressive groups collectively to fight the conservative machine. Instead, they are so embedded into the fabric and governance of the party that they cling to each bit of political turf and the power it provides. Their cacophony of noise—their uncoordinated messages on behalf of their individual causes—has prevented the party from developing and articulating a clear, concise, and all-encompassing vision that can serve as an antidote to the Republican worldview. In business parlance, there is no "elevator pitch" equivalent of the Democratic brand. And perhaps worst of all, these groups are blind to the harm that the Democratic Party's electoral setbacks of the last thirty years—and their complicity in those failures—have done to the very causes they hold dear.

Whatever successes they had were in the 1960s and 1970s, for too long now these single-issue groups have been fighting not to advance their causes, but to stop the backslide. They were already on the defensive for most of the 1980s and 1990s. But in this decade, with Republican domination of the executive, legislative, and judicial branches of the federal government, it's been shock-and-awe time. We're losing on almost every single issue—global warming, civil liberties, worker protections, abortion rights, the list goes on—while the conservatives are opening new battlefronts with creationism, antigay legislation, media consolidation, and so on. It's time we recognize that the way we have been doing business is not working anymore.

DIVIDED WE FALL

These single-issue groups not only hurt the Democratic Party in its search for a common identity, but they help provide the Republicans with a treasure trove of attack opportunities. While the Democratic Party should be the party of people, it has become, with a lot of help from Republican framing, a party of "immoral" abortionists, "extremist" tree-huggers, "corrupt" labor officials, "greedy" trial lawyers, "predatory" homosexuals, and "antiwhite" minority activists. After all, these *are* the loudest and most influential voices in our party—pro-choice groups, environmentalists, labor unions, trial lawyers, and identity groups. So it's not a stretch for demagogic Republicans to paint Democrats as a loose collection of selfish people who are fanatical about their specific cause and have no larger concerns—for the economy, the military, or the country.

That's not the case with the conservative movement's issue groups, which seem to operate from outside the party structure. We can talk about Grover Norquist, president of Americans for Tax Reform, and his control over the conservative movement, but it's the movement he controls, not the Republican Party. He exerts his enormous influence on the Republican agenda from the outside, and from behind the scenes. It's the same with Christian conservatives like Pat Robertson and James Dobson.

But on our side, the issue groups and the identity groups *are* the Democratic Party. And the problem is not just the categories and the segmentation, but the mind-sets they represent—there is too much emphasis on what the party can do for them and not enough on what they can do for the party.

If you want to see the problem up close, all you have to do is put a bunch of progressives together in the same room.

In April 2005, we had a chance to see just that, when about a hundred progressive leaders descended on Monterey, California, including such movement luminaries as syndicated columnist Arianna Huffington; Kim Gandy, president of the National Organization for Women; Maggie Fox, the deputy director of the Sierra Club; Wes Boyd and Joan Blades of MoveOn; Chellie Pingree, president of Common Cause; and Deborah Rappaport. The organizers from the Center for a New American Dream hoped to extract lessons from the 2004 election debacle while finding ways for progressives to move forward. It was a worthy endeavor, and one that offered rare networking opportunities between progressive leaders.

But it was also Exhibit A in the "Why Democrats Will Never Win" file. It was a prime example of a divided party, a split movement.

The conference was full of the silly group-building exercises that seem to infect all such gatherings, and had no shortage of reality-addled liberals. You know the type—the ones that believe we should just "visualize world peace," as though Somali warlords, Iraqi insurgents, or Colombian drug lords will simply vaporize if we just visualize. But the most obnoxious were the earnest practitioners of the single-issue dogma, the high priests and priestesses of that One Issue Everyone Must Care About Right Now. If everyone doesn't immediately sign on to their particular cause this instant, there will likely be immeasurable death and destruction and the world may come to an end. Over the past few decades these single-issue dogmatists have enforced their agendas by seeing who can yell the loudest. It was precisely these folks who spent a panel discussion on "building the progressive movement" giving each other high fives for what they considered a great victory in Rhode Island the month before.

Except that what happened in Rhode Island was not a victory, it was a setback—a direct result of the "cause-first, party-second" phenomenon. For the 2006 election, Senate Democrats had cast a net for candidates to take on the most endangered Republican Senate incumbents, and at the top of the list was Lincoln Chafee, a Republican anomaly in the most Democratic state in the union: Rhode Island.

Early polls showed U.S. Representative Jim Langevin, a former Rhode Island secretary of state, as close to a sure-thing winner against Chafee as was possible in the state that consistently gave Bush his worst approval ratings of all fifty states in Survey USA's monthly tracking poll; in December 2005, it was 25 percent. A Brown University poll in February 2005 gave Langevin a shocking 41 to 27 percent lead over Chafee, who was appointed to his father's seat in 1999 and elected in 2000. A month earlier, the partisan Democratic Senatorial Campaign Committee (DSCC) poll gave Langevin a 52 to 32 percent lead—any incumbent polling less than 50 percent is considered in potential danger.

With numbers like these, we could've sewn up that election and moved on to other tough battles. This seemed a lock for Langevin, and it seemed obvious that a Democrat—any Democrat—would be preferable to a Republican for progressive organizations. But Langevin had one problem that suddenly made him persona non grata to a segment of the party base—he has voted to restrict abortions. He opposed legislation that would have allowed women to obtain abortions at overseas military facilities using their own money, and voted for the criminalization of transportation of minors across state lines for abortions without parental consent.

Two heavyweights of the pro-choice movement—NARAL Pro-Choice America and the National Organization for Women—

exploded over the potential of a Langevin candidacy. Kate Michelman, past president of NARAL, said, "Can you imagine recruiting people to run for the Senate with a record of opposition to affirmative action or to *Brown v. Board of Education*?"[15] Further complicating the issue was the fact that the Republican Chafee claimed to be pro-choice, and on paper, in the isolated world of the "key votes" on the NARAL "scorecard," he looked pretty good on the abortion issue (with a score of 100% no less, compared to Langevin's 10%).

Here's where things get complicated. We want an America where a woman, not the government, has control over her own body. We want a world where a woman's doctor, not the theocons, can care for her reproductive health. We support the party that has enshrined abortion rights into its platform, not the party that has vowed to criminalize it. And who is in a better position to protect those rights—a lone pro-choice Republican or two within a governing party hell-bent on destroying those rights, or a lone antiabortion Democrat or two in a governing party determined to protect those rights? For the pro-choice groups, electing a Democratic majority that will build a progressive movement had to take a back seat to their own narrow agenda. They quickly mobilized a media blitz to oppose Langevin. Donors were recruited for supporting a primary challenger to Langevin.

In late March 2005 Langevin withdrew from the Senate race, saying he'd be more effective for Rhode Island building seniority in the House, but there was probably another factor involved in his calculations. Langevin would have had to go through a bruising and expensive primary battle with the pro-choice groups campaigning against him, and then start all over again to take on Chafee. While Chafee still remains one of the most endangered Republican incumbents in the Senate, both of his Democratic challengers, Sheldon Whitehouse and Matt Brown, trailed far behind Chafee in the polls as of October 2005. A race that appeared to be a slam dunk for the

Democrats was converted into a difficult (and more expensive) pickup opportunity.

Then, to add insult to that injury, NARAL gave Chafee an early endorsement in May 2005 over his two pro-choice Democratic rivals. That endorsement was given despite the fact that Chafee voted for Bill Frist as Senate Majority Leader (2004 NARAL scorecard: 0%) of a Republican Party with just two pro-choice senators (Chafee and Maine's Olympia Snowe). Even worse, weeks after NARAL's endorsement, Chafee voted with his party to confirm wingnut judge Janice Rogers Brown to the federal appeals court in D.C. And where does Judge Brown stand on reproductive rights? None other than NARAL said she was widely known as the "most conservative justice" on the California court. "Her hostility to reproductive rights, her ultra-conservative ideology, and her lack of judicial temperament demonstrate that Janice Rogers Brown would be a troubling addition to the federal judiciary," wrote NARAL.[16]

Antiabortion Democrat Harry Reid voted *against* Brown, probably based on other, nonchoice factors (including party loyalty), and Langevin likely would have as well. All but one Democrat voted against her. No Republican opposed her—not even Chafee, NARAL's darling and candidate of choice—and Brown was confirmed on a 56-43 vote. Judge Brown is now fit to fight abortion and other privacy rights (as well as other progressive principles) from her perch on the federal bench for the next twenty to forty years, long after Chafee leaves the Senate.

Ultimately, the election of every political candidate for office is about more than any single issue, even abortion rights. And while we disagreed with Langevin on abortion, there was plenty there for any good progressive to like. As a Democratic representative in the U.S. House, Langevin voted against the Iraq War, against the federal amendment banning same-sex marriages, and against the restrictions on bankruptcy sought by credit-card companies. He voted to require

DNA testing before all federal executions. The National Education Association, the AFL-CIO, the League of Conservation Voters, and the American Retirees Association all rated him 100% in 2004. He was given an "F" by the National Rifle Association in 2004 and received a low 34% from the right-wing U.S. Chamber of Commerce. And most surprising perhaps, this "antiwoman" politician scored perfect on every issue (other than abortion) on the scorecard of the American Association of University Women for the 108th Congress.

Was Langevin perfect? No, but who is? What candidate passes every single litmus test? No one, not even giants of the progressive movement like Russ Feingold, or Paul Wellstone, or Barbara Boxer. The fact remains that Langevin would likely never have gotten a chance to vote against abortion in a Democratic-led Senate, and otherwise would've been a huge boon to the larger progressive cause.

One of the mistakes we liberals make when looking across the aisle at our opponents is to think that they are a unified borg, a single-minded, single-purpose, smooth-functioning machine. It can be a source of great distress to contemplate, especially compared to the dysfunctional hodgepodge of competing agendas that make up the always-frayed progressive coalition. Yet one of the triumphs of the modern conservative movement has been the taming of their interest groups and their ability to get most of them on the same page most of the time. And it's not because (as some liberals like to think) they're all automatons who wake up each morning ready to take their marching orders. We've discussed these broad groups in the first chapter, but here, it's instructive to take a quick look at how they do it, because despite the inherent conflicts between the Republican-aligned groups, there is an appreciation for the broader conservative movement that has helped minimize the fault lines among them.

Back in 1994, Newt Gingrich was putting the finishing touches on his ten-point Contract with America, a document to be sprung in the closing weeks of the midterm elections that would present the nation with a tangible, governing blueprint for the conservative agenda.

Ralph Reed, then president of the Christian Coalition, demanded that Gingrich turn over one of the ten points to him, allowing the Contract to also address those "moral values" voters the Christian Coalition was motivating and turning out for Republican candidates nationwide. Gingrich refused, saying, in so many words, "Look Ralph, don't worry about it. You sell this to your flock and when we take over Congress, we'll take care of your issues." The rest, of course, is history. Gingrich helped sweep out the long-entrenched Democratic majority in the House.

Reed didn't just give Gingrich tacit approval. The Christian Coalition spent over $1 million promoting the Contract, and added untold hours of volunteer work for Republican candidates.[17] In early 1995, on a live Christian Coalition satellite broadcast to its chapters nationwide, a caller expressed concern that the Coalition was pushing Gingrich's Contract agenda but not saying much about abortion. Reed assured the caller that the Coalition would be "one of the clarion voices in American politics on behalf of that issue." And then he added this: "Right now, of course, . . . we're gonna be dealing with the Contract with America, which is welfare reform, term limits, tax cuts, a balanced budget amendment, and deficit reduction. We think every one of those issues affects the family, and we're gonna work on it."[18] Whatever else you might think about Reed, and he's an ideologue of the worst kind, politically speaking, he understood that when the movement wins, his causes win too.

Gingrich eventually repaid Reed's favor by publicly backing the Christian Coalition's Contract with the American Family, which included the usual antiabortion, antigay, anti-arts, and antiscience laundry list. Plus tax cuts.[19] Could liberals also put aside their pet causes in the name of the broader progressive movement? Could liberals get away from the laundry lists and litmus tests in the service of

a big-tent progressive majority, one in which their causes would
flourish?

If the Monterey conference was any indication, things don't look
so hot.

At one point, the conference split off into working groups to learn
practical steps for effectuating an advocacy campaign. It was meant
to be a how-to guide for progressive organizations, a lesson in coalition building, communication strategies, and goal setting. At one of
these breakout sessions, Andy Grossman of Wal-Mart Watch was
scheduled to speak about its collaboration and alliance-building
efforts. But from the beginning the session ran into problems. One
participant's hand shot up: "This isn't speaking to my issue. When are
we going to talk about *my* issue?" That set off an avalanche of copycat
complaints—"What about *my* issue?"—from all corners of the room.
To make a long and painful story short, a group of about forty people
scheduled to learn about effective *coalition building* split into five new
groups, all with a handful of people discussing *their* particular issue.
The bane of the progressive movement had struck—the demand by
single-issue groups to focus on their issue to the exclusion of anything
else. Even for one hour, in a session about working with other groups,
they were unable to pay attention to any issue but their own.

In our travels across the country, we interviewed dozens of people,
virtually all of whom pointed to the issue groups as serious problems
for the Democratic Party—a rare common thread among Democrats
inside and outside the D.C. beltway. Given how little these groups
are publicly criticized inside Democratic circles, it was a decidedly
unexpected sentiment. These advocacy groups are creatures of a different era. They were effective powerhouses in their heyday, partly
because the Democrats were in power and could get things done in
Congress, the White House, and even the courts. The civil rights
movement was singularly successful, the women's groups' efforts to
legalize abortion gave us *Roe v. Wade* in 1973, and the environmental

groups not only got landmark legislation passed—the Clean Water Act, the Clean Air Act, the Endangered Species Act, and so on—but they did a lot of that on a Republican president's watch. They even got President Richard Nixon to create the Environmental Protection Agency in 1970.

And then something happened—the clock kept turning, the times changed, people changed, but inertia set in among these established progressive organizations. They stood still, using what had proven to be successful formulas for legislative and public policy victories. In many ways, these organizations were victims of their own success. Conservative groups, being new and in the minority, were far more willing to experiment and work with new tactics and technologies. As they became more effective, their progressive counterparts failed to keep pace.

We could forgive the issue groups their dogged uncompromising fealty to their causes if it proved successful. But that hasn't been the case, at least not lately. And the successes of the past, no matter how glorious, are just that—the past. Not only is a determined conservative machine reversing those successes, but new successes have been scarce. It's worth taking a brief look at three of the major causes of the progressive movement (environmental issues, women's issues, and labor issues) to see what they have—or more accurately, what they have not—achieved in recent years.

"THE DEATH OF ENVIRONMENTALISM"

About a hundred years ago, John Muir, founder of the Sierra Club, wrote: "When we try to pick out anything by itself, we find it hitched to everything else in the universe." It was a prescient statement, and one that should apply to the entire progressive movement. But even today's environmentalists have strayed from a holistic approach to protecting our world, and simply offer a laundry list of issues.

In a highly influential and incendiary essay presented at the October 2004 meeting of the Environmental Grantmakers Association, Michael Shellenberger and Ted Nordhaus sparked a much-needed public discussion about the direction of the environmental movement. Appropriately titled "The Death of Environmentalism," the essay pointed out, among other things, that the way the movement was operating was not producing any results, and by way of example, they used the movement's failures regarding global warming, which has been a major priority lately. "Over the last 15 years environmental foundations and organizations have invested hundreds of millions of dollars into combating global warming. We have strikingly little to show for it," wrote Shellenberger and Nordhaus. "From the battles over higher fuel efficiency for cars and trucks to the attempts to reduce carbon emissions through international treaties, environmental groups repeatedly have tried and failed to win national legislation that would reduce the threat of global warming. As a result, people in the environmental movement today find themselves politically less powerful than we were one and a half decades ago."

One major failure for the environmental movement came with the Senate rejection of the Kyoto Protocol of 1997, an international treaty on climate change aimed at greatly reducing global-warming gasses. The Senate passed a resolution opposing U.S. participation in the treaty by an astonishing 95-0 vote, a stunning political loss for an environmental community focused on policy prescriptions as a solution to every environmental ill. Neither Bill Clinton nor George W. Bush has even submitted the treaty to the Senate for ratification. Other failures of the environmental movement have had objectively disastrous results. Hurricane Katrina had a far more devastating effect on the Gulf Coast than would have otherwise been the case without the destruction of the coastal wetlands of Louisiana that have traditionally acted as hurricane speed bumps.

Ronald Reagan was bad enough for the environment, once famously stating that "trees cause more pollution than automobiles," but Bush is even worse. A story in the September 2005 *Rolling Stone* magazine by Tim Dickinson had this appropriate headline: "A Polluter's Feast: Bush has reversed more environmental progress in the past eight months than Reagan did in a full eight years." Among the list of setbacks mentioned was that the Bush administration "allowed the import of methyl bromide, a cancer-causing pesticide that was due to be banned this year under an international accord signed by Ronald Reagan." A full accounting of the environmental backslide during the Bush administration has been well documented by the National Resources Defense Council and others, but aside from the usual fare about logging, drilling, and mining in protected national forests and the weakening of clean air and water restrictions, there are some particularly egregious failures.[20]

For example, at the urging of the chemical industry, the EPA now allows the testing of pesticides on humans. A report by California Democrats senator Barbara Boxer and representative Henry Waxman stated: "Reversing a moratorium established by the Clinton Administration, the Environmental Protection Agency under the Bush Administration is reviewing or plans to review over 20 studies that intentionally dosed human subjects with pesticides. The pesticides administered to human subjects in these experiments include 'highly hazardous' poisons, suspected carcinogens, and suspected neurotoxicants. The studies, most of which were submitted to EPA by pesticide manufacturers, appear to routinely violate ethical standards."[21] This is a morally repugnant "research" that targets the desperately poor. The *Washington Post* reported on June 28, 2005, that: "Under the draft rule, the EPA could still accept some studies involving children, pregnant women and newborns, and it would not establish an independent ethics review board to scrutinize human studies on the grounds that this would 'unnecessarily confine EPA's discretion.' The agency would allow testing pesticides on humans to determine at what level they become toxic. This could include tests on prisoners even though they might be 'vulnerable to coercion or undue influence,' the draft rule states."

So the assault on the environment and its devastating public health consequences continues, leaving the environmental groups feebly protesting each new setback.

Similar to our research-related travels, Shellenberger and Nordhaus held lengthy discussions with nearly all the leaders from major environmental organizations, many of whom insisted that the environmental movement was still on track. "Not one of America's environmental leaders is articulating a vision of the future commensurate with the magnitude of the crisis," wrote Shellenberger and Nordhaus. "Instead they are promoting technical policy fixes like pollution controls and higher vehicle mileage standards—proposals that provide neither the popular inspiration nor the political alliances the community needs to deal with the problem. By failing to question their most basic assumptions about the problem and the solution, environmental leaders are like generals fighting the last war—in particular the war they fought and won for basic environmental protections more than 30 years ago."

To their detriment, progressive organizations feel comfortable advocating policy-based solutions to problems. Meanwhile, the other side is waging an ideological war. Their narrative is the protection of the American way of life, the creation of jobs, the growing of the economy, the march of progress. The environmental movement has no competing narrative, only narrow "policy fixes"—restricting the timber industry to save the spotted owl, reining in the oil industry to keep the Alaskan Arctic National Wildlife Refuge pristine, forcing fuel-efficiency standards on the automobile companies to protect the ozone layer, and so on. There is no effort to create a broader narrative that would embrace these issues and generate sympathy and support for environmentalism in general as a common good. Or as Deborah Rappaport put it, "It's not just about saving the tree frog in Oregon, it's about why environmentalism matters in a more global sense."

As Shellenberger and Nordhaus note, "the environmental community's narrow definition of its self-interest leads to a kind of policy literalism that undermines its power. . . . When you look at the long string of global warming defeats under Presidents Bill Clinton and George W. Bush, it is hard not to conclude that the environmental movement's approach to problems and policies hasn't worked particularly well. And yet there is nothing about the behavior of environmental groups, and nothing in our interviews with environmental leaders, that indicates that we as a community are ready to think differently about our work."

One reason why there may not be enough incentive to reform and to "think differently about our work" is that most of the leading environmental groups are quite entrenched in their ways—and are still supremely well funded. They're not the hungry young activists of the 1960s. In 2004, the Sierra Club had an annual budget of $100 million and 750,000 members; the National Resources Defense Council had revenues of $55 million and about 1 million members; Greenpeace USA had an $18-million budget (for 2003) and about 250,000 members (2.5 million worldwide); Environmental Defense had $50 million and 400,000 members; the Audubon Society had $74 million and 500,000 members; and the National Wildlife Federation had $118 million and 800,000 members. This is an incomplete list of environmental groups. And despite the hundreds of millions of dollars spent each year by these groups, they are stuck in neutral at best, with one foot on the brake so they don't slide back.

Until the environmental community taps into a broader progressive ideology and sells *that* to the public in alliance with the other progressive causes and groups, it will likely continue to see its every policy initiative defeated.

THE DECLINE OF LABOR

An old International Workers of the World (a.k.a. the Wobblies) poster features a car carrying a bunch of cats. A fat cat drives the car while three or four smaller cats sit in the back. The cats in the back, looking at the lone driver, say, "There's so many of us and there's so few of them." The labor movement is potentially the most broad-based of the progressive groups since it is about workplace issues, but despite the words of that Wobblies' poster, there are just not that many cats remaining under the union banner.

In the mid-1950s, 35 percent of the American wage-and-salary workforce was organized under a union. That figure declined to 25 percent by 1974.[22] Today, it stands at 12.5 percent, with only 8.5 percent of private sector employees in a union, both figures declining each year.[23] And like all other groups in the Democratic coalition, labor is suffering serious setbacks on all issues that matter to workers.

Nowadays, Wal-Mart is ground zero for the labor movement. Both sides work as if their existence depends on the outcome, and in many ways, it might. Wal-Mart has built its empire on the backs of its 1.7 million workers, the most of any company in the country.[24] It has topped the Fortune 500 the last three years (2002–05) in revenue (joining General Motors and ExxonMobil as the only companies ever to top the list created in 1954).[25] Wal-Mart had $288 billion in sales in 2004, with $10.3 billion in net income. It represents the twenty-sixth largest economy in the world, and is China's sixth largest trading partner—among businesses and countries. And yet, American-owned and operated, its average wage in 2005 was around $10 an hour. Subtract highly compensated company executives and the average drops to $8.50 an hour, or $14,000 a year, about $2,000 below the already ridiculously low federal poverty level for a family of three.[26]

Wal-Mart offers lessons to employees on applying for government healthcare, since it refuses to cover the bulk of its own workforce, making itself a beneficiary of corporate welfare. It is virulently antiunion, as one of its manager handbooks, "You and Your Labor Relations, What a Wal-Mart Supervisor Should Know about Labor Unions" makes clear:

> Staying union free is a full-time commitment. Unless union prevention is a goal equal to other objectives within an organization, the goal will usually not be attained. The commitment to stay union free must exist at all levels of management—from the Chairperson of the "Board" down to the front-line manager. Therefore, no one in management is immune to carrying his or her "own weight" in the union prevention effort. The entire management staff should fully comprehend and appreciate exactly what is expected of their individual efforts to meet the union-free objective. . . . Unless each member of management is willing to spend the necessary time, effort, energy, and money, it will not be accomplished. The time involved is . . . 365 days per year. . . .[27]

What's most terrifying to labor is that other American corporations are embracing Wal-Mart as a model of success. If Wal-Mart succeeds in its union-resisting ways, how does the labor movement stay relevant? How can the unions bust Wal-Mart's model, forcing it to advance the living standards of its workers, and set an example for the rest of corporate America?

One of the point men in the battle against Wal-Mart is Paul Blank, formerly the national political director of Howard Dean's presidential campaign and now the campaign director for WakeUpWalmart.com, a project of the United Food and Commercial Workers International Union. When we talked with him at union headquarters in Washington, D.C., in June 2005, he summed up one of the biggest challenges facing a labor movement trying to stay relevant in a country increasingly enamored with cheap consumer products that are the result of outsourcing jobs abroad. "How do you create a movement out of nothing other than people who think that it's wrong to pay people below-poverty-level wages?" Blank asks. "They think it's wrong not to provide health insurance, think it's wrong to use child labor and sweat shops and all that kind of stuff. They definitely think all those things are wrong, but they also like getting a $3 refrigerator."

The "$3 refrigerator" is a reference to Jon Stewart's line on *The Daily Show*, when he said of Wal-Mart: "You could say they've destroyed the fabric of small-town America. On the other hand, $3 FOR A REFRIGERATOR!" And those aren't made in the USA. The parts necessary to build them aren't built here either. Consumer appetite for low prices has fueled the demise of American manufacturing with predictable devastation to the labor movement. So reversing the failing fortunes of labor is critical, not just for labor itself, but for the entire Democratic Party.

Richard Yeselson is a longtime union hand and current senior research analyst at UNITE-HERE, a newly merged union of restaurant, hotel, textile, and industrial workers. Yeselson has seen the twin attacks on labor by the Wal-Marts of the corporate world and by a Bush administration catering to its corporate sponsors. "The first thing that Bush did—I mean this was literally the very first act of his presidency—was to roll back Clinton's ergonomic rules which had been worked out over ten years," Yeselson told us at the National Building Museum in D.C. in June 2005. "Union members are aware of that because unions have worker health and safety committees. So even if you're not a particularly active union member, you know what your Health and Safety Committee is doing. And the rule would have improved the lives of millions of nonunion workers too, another example of how the labor movement has so often fought to improve the lives of nonunion members—starting with Social Security, civil rights, minimum wage legislation, many other issues."

It's hard to imagine now, but labor used to be one of the most integral parts of the U.S. economy and of American life in general.

Yeselson quizzed us: "The great steel strike of 1959 was *the* story in America for weeks. President Eisenhower had to intervene to settle it. Do you know why?" We had no clue. "Because all steel plants were in this country, not Korea or Russia. No steel, no cars, no bombs and bullets—we weren't fighting a war then. We're talking about 500,000 steelworkers who could basically stop the American economy—it was the largest strike in the history of the United States."

Of all the constituency groups we're discussing, labor probably has the most damaged brand of the lot. During the 1950s and 1960s, organized labor lost much of the energy and sense of purpose that helped it grow during the New Deal and postwar era. Labor's reputation for social idealism was tarnished by the infiltration of some unions by organized crime elements. Senate hearings investigating the Teamsters and its president, Jimmy Hoffa, riveted the nation in 1957 and 1958; the 1954 Academy Award–winning film, *On the Waterfront*, dramatically depicted this corruption, with Marlon Brando memorably playing the role of a dockworker who informs on his corrupt union bosses.

At around the same time, union membership failed to keep up with the growth in the workforce, slowed by complacency and by overwhelming opposition to organizing in the fast-growing South. Labor then missed a huge opportunity to lend its organizational muscle and organizing savvy to the emerging movements—of students, women, blacks, and antiwar Americans—during the sixties and early seventies. Cultural differences divided working-class union members from the growing middle-class-led progressive social movements of the era.

By 1972, the AFL-CIO's Vietnam War–supporting leadership thumbed its nose at George McGovern's antiwar platform and, for the only time in its history, did not endorse the Democratic candidate for president. (Ironically, McGovern had a Ph.D. in American labor history, writing his dissertation on the famous Ludlow, Colorado, coal miners massacre).

Today, labor appears more of an anachronism than a vibrant component of the modern progressive movement. It's obvious to many labor union leaders, says Blank, that "doing the same thing—the status quo—cannot stand. That's a path to nowhere. A lot of the labor groups are having to look in the mirror and recognize that they either change or they die. . . . Some people see it and want to stay the same because it works for them. And other people see it and want to change, but they don't necessarily agree on how to change."

Labor unions are at a crossroads. Their numbers are declining rapidly, their causes are under assault from a hostile administration, the Wal-Mart economy threatens to steamroll them into oblivion, and yet they know that they are fighting the good fight. The real challenge for labor is in how it deploys its resources. Does it redirect money and manpower toward aggressively organizing new workplaces and growing its ranks? Does it plow more money into the Democratic Party and its pro-labor candidates and become an even bigger player in that party? Does it hedge its bets and begin to make more donations to moderate Republicans?

Those and other questions and challenges led to the first major split in the labor movement since 1935, with the Service Employees International Union (SEIU)*, the largest union in the country with 1.3 million members, joining the Teamsters in leading a splinter group away from the AFL-CIO during, ironically, the fiftieth-anniversary celebration of the merger between the AFL and CIO. At

---

*Jerome is a consultant for SEIU's internet operations.

the heart of the separation, which took place in Chicago in October 2005, was a division of opinion over the direction of activism dollars. The AFL-CIO insisted on the status quo, directly funding the Democratic Party and its candidates as it did to the tune of nearly $54 million in 2004 (with another $8 million going to Republicans).[28] Some of the rebel unions argued that this money should be used for organizing and rebuilding their depleted ranks. For some of the groups that splintered, the change of direction was essential to begin growing their ranks through organizing efforts—only then could labor have the numerical strength to leverage political change.

For the Democratic Party, a strong labor force translates into victory at the ballot box. Traditionally the "workhorses" of progressive politics, labor groups also provide cash, canvassing, and "get out the vote" (GOTV) operations for the Democratic Party. Union members generally vote Democratic, so growing their ranks has huge implications for the future of the progressive movement and the Democratic Party. For every three members that labor unions create, they add two new Democratic voters. In 2004, gun owners voted for Bush over Kerry by 20 percent, but gun owners who belonged to a union chose Kerry by 12 percent. Overall, white men chose Bush by 13 percent, but white male union voters preferred Kerry by 21 percent. Overall, union members voted for Kerry 65 to 33 percent, giving him a net advantage of 5.8 million votes.[29]

While it might be easy to get caught up with the emergence of the netroots effort, and think the internet holds the answer to everything that ails Democrats, it's currently difficult to reach a large chunk of working-class Americans without labor's help. These union members are not engaging in politics online, or are not engaged at all, and can be swayed by the Right's culture-war attacks on the Democrats to the detriment of their own economic well-being.

If labor unions can begin to build alliances with the rest of the progressive groups and begin to articulate their concerns in the language of morality and basic human rights—a living wage, access to health care, workplace protections, and so on—they can be a major force in helping revive the progressive movement, and the Democratic Party as well.

A WOMAN'S RIGHT TO LOSE?

Few groups have become as stuck in the past as the pro-choice movement. While dealing with one of the most ethically complex and heart-wrenching issues facing our society, these groups continue to work off their 1970s handbook, refusing to acknowledge the moral component of the issue and seeing it as simply a legal and legislative battle. While abortion has remained generally safe and legal the past three decades, antichoice activists have chipped away at those protections.

Abortion is available now in only 13 percent of U.S. counties. Bush Jr. has already placed over 200 new antiabortion judges on the federal bench. The nation's views on abortion are gradually shifting to the right. A July 2005 poll by the Pew Research Center showed that while 65 percent of adults would not want to see the Supreme Court completely overturn *Roe v. Wade*, only 35 percent supported no limits on abortion and just 26 percent thought the issue was "not a moral issue."

One reason for the shift in public opinion is that the leaders of the pro-choice movement have failed to adapt to the changing times. Sarah Blustain, a deputy editor at *The American Prospect*, wrote a controversial December 6, 2004, piece in her magazine entitled "Choice Language," challenging Democrats to rethink the way they talk about abortion. "As long as I can remember, the tone of the liberal message on abortion has been defiant, sometimes even celebratory," Blustain wrote. "It's an attitude that reflects the victory of legal abortion over back-alley dangers three decades ago—a success that many who remember it still experience with deep emotion." And those activists still see abortion as simply a legal issue, and they see the legality of the "right to choose" as a reason for celebration.

"For those of us who came after *Roe v. Wade*, there is a significantly different reality. The context has changed," wrote Blustain. "Back alleys and coat hangers are not part of our visceral memory. To this generation, the 'choice' of a legal abortion is no longer something to celebrate. It is a decision made in crisis, and it is never one made happily. Have you ever talked to a woman who has had an abortion? Even a married, intentionally pregnant woman who has had a 'D and C' for a dying or dead embryo? A college student whose birth control failed? I promise you, such a woman does not talk about exercising the 'right to choose.' You may accuse her—and me—of taking such rights for granted, and maybe you'd be right. But mainly she will tell you how sad she is, how she wished she hadn't had to make that 'choice,' how unpleasant the procedure was. She is more likely depressed than defiant."

It is not inconsistent to recognize, on the one hand, that women have an inalienable right to control their bodies and their reproductive organs, while at the same time to acknowledge that abortions represent a failure—whether of judgment, of genetics, of equipment, or of economics—and that they are viscerally disturbing procedures. To frame what is a fundamentally unpleasant act as just a "choice" or even a "right" seems insensitive to the emotional toll of having an abortion. Such an act can't be reduced to the language of law or consumerism. For the old-guard pro-choice activist, it was the language of liberation. But the times have changed; the issue is no longer black and white. Blustain quotes Cynthia Gorney, author of *Articles of Faith: A Frontline History of the Abortion Wars*, saying, "The way that the advocacy groups have organized themselves . . . has been all or nothing."

Blustain echoes that sentiment, adding that abortion is not "like women's suffrage or the equal access to public accommodations, rights whose outcome is emotionally unambiguous. The vocabulary that was so powerful in the 1950s, '60s, and '70s means something different today. The national debates—on welfare, on affirmative action, and, yes, on abortion—have underscored the nuances. The question no longer seems as simple as, 'Are you for or against?' We are for. But how are we for, to what extent, and at what cost?"

Moral ambiguities abound. Is a twenty-four-hour waiting period a reasonable restriction for a major personal decision, or an unnecessary obstacle? Is requiring teenagers to notify parents before having an abortion an unfair or dangerous burden on the pregnant teen or an abandonment of parental rights? Does support for such restrictions represent a denial of a woman's right to choose, or are there shades of gray in an exceedingly complex ethical issue? Does it have to be all or nothing? The demands of 100 percent allegiance to an absolutist view of abortion rights may very well be costing us, not just today, but also in the long term.

A Gallup poll conducted in August 2003 showed that 72 percent of teens thought abortion was morally wrong, 32 percent thought abortion should be illegal, and 47 percent thought there should be restrictions—all numbers more hostile to abortion than among adult respondents. And it's not that teens are becoming more socially conservative. Other Gallup polls conducted around the same time period showed that teens supported affirmative action 56 to 40 percent, approved of gay marriages 55 to 42 percent, and gay adoption 51 to 46 percent, all far above the comparable rates of adults. Progressives have gained on social issues such as equality and diversity, but are losing ground over abortion rights.

Abortion rights are in danger if a whole generation of Americans is growing up hostile to the core precepts of the pro-choice movement. Yet the pro-choice groups continue to operate almost exactly as they did in the 1970s—same language and tactics. A simple tactical shift emphasizing the goal of reducing unwanted pregnancies as well as defending the right to choose would bring many into the fold who view abortion with some distaste but want to keep abortion safe and legal. And even while the Republican stampede of the last few years threatens the right to abortion, these groups insist on a level of Democratic purity that ultimately harms their own interests. They cling to the fiction that a politician's stated position on abortion is the single most important issue that matters to women—or even the broader progressive movement.

Earlier we mentioned the Rhode Island Senate race controversy over the matter of abortion and how Representative Langevin withdrew after pro-choice groups opposed him. Pennsylvania has a similar 2006 Senate race, where antiabortion Democrat Bob Casey is the heavy favorite to oust bona fide wingnut Rick Santorum. A Casey victory would get us one seat closer to retaking the Senate and creating a firewall against the Republican radical right-wing agenda, yet women's groups have been actively hostile to him. NOW president Kim Gandy claimed that Democrats were "abandoning women" and called Casey "a danger to our cause." Martha Burk, chairwoman of the National Council of Women's Organizations, said "in terms of women's lives, what difference does it make whether we have a pro-life Democrat or a pro-life Republican?"[30]

Well, as the Chafee/Langevin example showed, there is clearly a big difference between who ends up in the Senate leadership posts, the kind of judges a senator will vote to approve, and the kind of legislation that will come to a vote. And while Santorum has written a book arguing that young women shouldn't be encouraged to go to college and that women should stay home and not work, Casey has used his treasurer's office in Pennsylvania to promote women's issues, including women-owned businesses.

The National Council of Women's Organizations publishes a handy guide to women's issues[31] and it lists a host of topics that are of great concern to women, besides abortion: child care, early childhood education, family leave, affirmative action, access to contraception, health insurance and access to health care, political participation, workplace pay equity, Social Security, prohibiting discrimination in education, stopping violence against women, effective welfare reform, and job training and education. But Casey's record on these issues is trumped by his abortion stance. The fact that Casey would likely vote against many of the right-wing, reactionary, antiabortion judges Bush nominates (just as the antiabortion Harry Reid has done) is ignored. The fact that antiabortion legislation would never see the light of day in a Democratic-led Senate is also ignored.

The majority of Americans consider themselves "pro-choice." Survey USA tracking data through 2005 on abortion shows that nationwide, 56 percent of Americans consistently describe themselves as "pro-choice" while just 38 percent describe themselves as "pro-life."[32] That the choice community has failed to further safeguard abortion rights, while at the same time understanding how to deal with the moral ambiguity of the issue is the tactical failure. That it has refused to embrace the broader progressive movement as a way to protect its interests is the strategic failure.

NEW CAMPAIGNS, NEW MOVEMENT

The environmental, labor, and choice constituency groups aren't alone in their failures and their futility. The gun control groups are essentially dead. As for the various identity groups—based on race and ethnicity—they are still alive, but the issues important to them, like poverty, affirmative action, fair and affordable housing, racial profiling, school aid, immigration reform, and the like are filed under the "won't see daylight, ever" category in the basement of Republican headquarters. Gays are now the new national whipping post. The line between church and state continues to blur. Even groups that really have no business being politicized, like scientists and educators, are now forced to beat back right-wing attacks on science, research, and our nation's education system.

Though it's always had its critics, there was a time when the constituency group model worked, as Mark Schmitt wrote in October 2005 in a piece in *The American Prospect* entitled "We're All Environmentalists Now," commemorating the one-year anniversary of *Death of Environmentalism*. "Shellenberger and Nordhaus revealed a death, but it was not that of environmentalism as an idea. Rather, it is interest-group pluralism, the model of liberal advocacy under which all of us over 30 were raised, that is finished. . . . It worked reasonably well as a way for liberals with some share of power to allocate resources," Schmitt wrote. "And for particular issues, the environment in particular, interest-group pluralism gave that movement a broad base of support" beyond just a progressive audience.

But the Republican opposition has brought "interest-group pluralism to its knees. Pluralism is a strategy for making improvements while holding governing power; it is not a strategy to save the world from those with unchecked power."

The political landscape has shifted under Republican rule and marginalized Democrats. How any of these progressive groups can defend the status quo is hard to understand. That is, until you consider that even in the minority, even as their world crumbles around them, even as they keep losing ground, they retain a certain amount of power— or at least a façade of it. Senators and congressmen still take their calls. Candidates still covet their endorsements and fear their wrath because major campaign donors still look to the groups' stamps of approval. The press builds them up as representatives of millions of people. Their big funders still write their checks and their members still send in their annual dues. Yet at the end of the day, it's hard to build a movement or strengthen a political party when its constituency groups are tugging it in a dozen different directions.

But all is not lost. While Washington, D.C., may be stultified by archaic, status-quo thinking, the states are a hotbed of innovation. There are new, more authentic candidates rising up, there are new ways of redefining the Democratic party's relationship with the single-issue groups, and there are new multi-issue "movement" groups (and big donors) becoming more active and influential in progressive politics. And despite all of the Democratic losses in 2004 (and 2002 and 2000), we had some successes that laid to waste much of the D.C.-based conventional thinking. Each state is different, and the solutions can't be a "one size fits all" proposition, but one thing these successes had in common was a rejection of the "Democratic Party coalition" *mentality*. Gone was the notion that we could build to 50 percent-plus-one of the electorate by tallying African Americans (12 percent), Latinos (13 percent), union members (12 percent), pro-choice women (25 to 35 percent), gays, environmentalists, and presto! Instant majority!

Two of 2004's biggest Democratic success states—Colorado and Montana—approached the dilemma of the issue groups in completely different ways.

Colorado witnessed a Democratic tidal wave that swept out entrenched legislative Republicans, despite the heavy pro-GOP tilt of the national electorate in a state that Bush carried 52-47 over John Kerry.

And the root of that Democratic success was an unprecedented coordinated effort by single-issue progressive groups. They had, let's say, a certain *incentive* for playing along, for working in concert, for collaborating. It came in the form of four innovative funders, dubbed the "four horsemen": Jared Polis, best known for creating, then selling, the e-greeting card site BlueMountain.com to the Excite portal for $745 million in 1999; Rutt Bridges, an entrepreneur who earned his fortune creating software for the energy industry; Tim Gill, who founded Quark Inc., the industry-standard desktop publishing software-application firm; and Pat Stryker, whose source of wealth was in the medical-equipment business. They had the money. However, they needed ground troops, and who better than the advocacy groups? So the four funders spent over $2 million on a shadow campaign organization—separate from the Democratic Party—for get-out-the-vote and registration efforts in the 2004 election cycle.

ProgressNow's Michael Huttner chaired the Coalition for a Better Colorado, this new movement-based effort. When we talked with Huttner in Denver in June 2005, he told us that the first challenge was getting the single-issue groups to join the effort. "We had to pull these major interest groups together, and that was probably one of the biggest hurdles," Huttner said. "When you get these folks on the phone, they immediately start with the 'What ifs?' What if our person is pro-choice but not pro-labor? What if a candidate is pro-labor but not pro-choice—then you know the NARAL person doesn't want to get involved.

"So I said 'We're meeting next Wednesday at 2 p.m. in this room, and I'm not going to get into it on the phone, but if you want to be there, there will be representatives from all the key groups and a few major funders. Be there if you want.'"

Everyone showed up. Not only did these groups not want to be left out, but the "four horsemen" also happen to be major funders of many of these groups, and it was prudent to participate. And at that meeting, the groups and funders set up two political "527" organizations (named after the section in the IRS regulations that allows them to incorporate as nonprofits without regulation by the Federal Election Commission or similar state-based regulatory agencies)— Coalition for a Better Colorado and the Alliance for a Better Colorado. The Coalition was set up to help and support candidates that checked off every box in the liberal laundry list, which was 90 to 95 percent of the candidates they supported. The Alliance was designed to help Democrats who held positions that conflicted with one of the member issue groups, which accounted for the other 5 to

10 percent of candidates. No single issue group was required to fund a candidate whose positions conflicted with its core mission.

The plan was brilliant and, better yet, successful. The two umbrella groups split the Colorado map with clear zones of responsibility, focusing on the nuts and bolts of voter education, identifying progressive voters, and making sure they got to the polls. In short, they ran the ground operation, which allowed the Democratic Party itself to focus instead on message and candidate recruitment. The well-oiled, well-planned, and well-executed machine targeted sixteen state house seats and helped win fifteen of them. A 37-28 GOP advantage in the state house was turned into a 35-30 Democratic one. Democrats also picked up a state senate seat to take back that branch of the legislature as well, going from an 18-17 GOP edge to an 18-17 Democratic one. Democrat Ken Salazar also won 51-47, one of only two Democratic pickups in the U.S. Senate in 2004.

Lessons learned? Combining efforts works better than working in each group's silo. Working to make sure Democrats win control is more important than sabotaging the chances of any candidate that doesn't check off every box on the liberal laundry list.

Since the 2004 election, the architects of the Colorado plan have been in great demand, speaking around the country on the lessons to be learned from their experience. And while there are key logistical factors that contributed to their success, at the root it was a story about movement building. As a result, the Colorado legislature is now much friendlier to all of those issue-group's agendas, even if every Democrat in the governing majority doesn't support each specific group's respective agenda.

Montana was also a major Democratic success story of the 2004 elections—but with a completely different model. Montana Democrats nearly cut the issue groups out of their campaign efforts. They shocked the political world by winning four of five statewide elected offices, with rancher Brian Schweitzer leading the way with a

50-46 victory to become governor. At the same time, Montana was paying homage to its ultraconservative nature by giving Bush a solid 59-39 blowout. While we'll examine the "Montana Miracle" in greater detail later in the book, it's relevant to mention here that one of the key factors in the Democratic success was their complete divorce from Montana's progressive groups.

The first thing Schweitzer did when starting his uphill governor's run was *not* fill out those questionnaires issue groups love to send candidates to gauge their devotion to their particular causes—answer enough questions correctly and you might be eligible for some donations or an endorsement or both. "I threw all of the questionnaires in the garbage," Schweitzer told us at the state capitol in Helena, Montana, in July 2005. There was actually one exception—the National Rifle Association (NRA) questionnaire. "I filled that one out because you've got to fill that one out," he said. In a state where voters still thought that Democrats were out to take away their guns, Schweitzer felt he had to neutralize that charge. And the NRA was the most efficient vehicle to that end.

"In order to get an 'A plus,' you've got to shoot somebody," Schweitzer deadpanned. "And I was looking."

Rural Democrats all across the nation are still suffering the legacy of the now near-dead gun control groups, efforts that allowed the Republican noise machine to score striking propaganda victories at the expense of Democrats. A whole generation of libertarian-minded gun owners became solid Republicans to protect their prized weapons from Democratic efforts to pry them from their cold, dead fingers— the curse of the single-issue group at work. And Democrats like Schweitzer, Virginia governor Mark Warner, and DNC chairman Howard Dean all worked to reassure voters that Democrats had no design on taking away their guns.

But aside from the gun issue, Schweitzer was unwilling to let any constituency group force his hand on any issue, and the rest of the state's Democrats followed suit. It was a rare rebuke of the issue groups in the Democratic Party, but one that served the purposes of the long-suffering Montana Democratic Party. With separation from those groups, Schweitzer and the rest of the Democratic ticket in Montana could stand on their own, unencumbered by whatever negative baggage those groups might bring. The results were dramatic—a 53-47 deficit in the state house was turned into a 50-50 chamber with Democrats holding the tie-breaking vote. In the state senate, a 29-21 deficit became a 27-23 advantage. Now, progressive groups have a much friendlier state government in Helena than during the previous dark years of Republican domination.

So which is it? Do we take the constituency groups and mold them into a new powerhouse movement like in Colorado, or do we relegate them to the sidelines as in Montana? Much obviously depends on local conditions, and the more conservative a state is, the more Democrats might need to distance themselves from those very groups that have helped ruin the party's brand. But on a national level, it's clear that the model is both—the constituency groups must join the new and growing progressive movement, while keeping their distance from the Democratic Party's electoral apparatus.

The "Democratic Party coalition" of the past few decades has failed. It must be replaced by a new progressive movement, one that is dedicated to finding those common bonds that tie us together while tolerating the sorts of differences inevitable in any "big tent" gathering. And that movement needs to remain *outside* the party, giving Democratic candidates the freedom to get elected in all parts of the country without being smeared by association with any particular interest group.

This new movement is already on the rise. The McCain-Feingold campaign-finance reform law of 2002, cosponsored by Democratic senator Russ Feingold of Wisconsin and Republican senator John McCain of Arizona, was supposed to gut the Democratic Party and strip it of its main source of funding—unregulated million-dollar "soft money" donations. Yet the law had the opposite effect. A party addicted to million-dollar donations suddenly found itself forced to seek out small donors. The Republicans had no such problems. Despite popular conception to the contrary, it was the Republicans who had built a wide network of small-dollar donors to fund their operations. In fact, Republicans led Democrats in dollars raised for all groups except those over $1 million.

While establishment Democrats fretted that the McCain-Feingold bill would destroy their ability to compete with Republicans, a new generation of activists began to flex their muscles. MoveOn.org had built a three-million-strong membership list based on its defense of Clinton during his impeachment saga and later, its opposition to the Iraq War. Activists on websites like DemocraticUnderground.com and the emerging bloggers, including the two of us, focused netroots activists on specific races and various causes, and they began to raise money.

While the money captured the political and media establishment's attention, there is another important dynamic at work—these activists are not advocating just for any single issue or cause. This brand of political activism is not wedded to the past, when Democrats were a governing party and single-issue groups existed to promote their agendas in the halls of the Capitol. Rather, these activists have emerged at a time of Democrats being the minority power, where progressives and their causes have been relegated to the dustbin.

It's partly a generational shift, of liberals who grew up in the 1990s, not the 1960s or 1970s, not based on the age of the activist, but on the date of his or her entrance into the political arena. Prior to the mid-1990s, the political scene was dominated by single-issue groups. But in the last decade, every major new activist group has been multi-issue and movement-based: MoveOn.org, Democracy for America, the bloggers, the National Hip Hop Political Conference, think tanks like the Center for American Progress, and so on. And a new generation of big-dollar donors has emerged to fund many of these organizations, seeding the beginnings of a new Vast Left-Wing Conspiracy to rival the machine on the Right. These new political players are focused on building a dominant progressive majority, one in which everyone's favorite cause faces a friendly reception in the halls of government.

There is a growing understanding—still rare among established progressive political circles—that no one's narrow agenda is served by being in the minority and that a governing majority would mean far more for everyone's pet causes than a hostile, entrenched, dominant Republican majority. All the think tanks and white papers in the world are useless unless we are in the governing majority and can get those policies implemented.

Single-issue groups can be essential components of the larger movement. They can provide activists with action alerts and research to tackle issues, and they can energize their supporters in coordination with other field groups (as they did in Colorado). But they need not control the party and its candidates as they try to regain the majority.

Let the party be the party, with the movement outside looking in.

THE GRAVY TRAIN

"I don't get it. When a consultant on the Republican side loses, we take them out and shoot them. You guys—keep hiring them."

—Nationally prominent Republican official

It was 1998 and Democratic senator Russ Feingold of Wisconsin was locked in a battle for his political life. Elected to the U.S. Senate six years earlier, Feingold was being nationally targeted by the Republican Party, notably for pushing campaign finance reform. His Republican opponent, Representative Mark Neumann, was flush with cash, and the race was going down to the wire.

But Feingold had more than his Republican foes to worry about. The Democratic Party establishment was making his life difficult as well. Apparently Feingold wasn't running his campaign according to the script, and the party was determined to save the senator from himself. And as is the case with most political problems, money was involved. Feingold's crime, as the Democratic establishment saw it, was his refusal to accept political action committee (PAC) contributions or "soft money" expenditures by the Democratic Senatorial Campaign Committee (DSCC).

"[DSCC chair] Senator Bob Kerrey came up to me on the Senate floor and says, 'You don't want soft money?'" Feingold recounted when we met him in Washington, D.C., in June 2005. "I said 'No. I would rather lose than use unlimited contributions.' He said, 'Are you winking at me?'"

In a town full of winks and nods, Kerrey's question was understandable. But Feingold was dead serious. His position was one of extreme political courage, perhaps bordering on folly. Feingold's opponent had $11 million to work with, far outspending Feingold who had vowed not to spend more than $1 per eligible voter—about $4 million in all. But whether Feingold wanted it or not, the DSCC was determined to help him. "In the last couple of weeks, the DSCC decided to run these vicious attack ads on my opponent," Feingold said. "Of course, who is going to believe that I wasn't part of this effort? So I was finishing a debate in Green Bay and I called up Kerrey and I called up everybody and I said 'These have got to stop!' because it undercut my credibility completely." Feingold eventually went to Democratic Senate leader Tom Daschle who then went to Kerrey and had the ads pulled. But the D.C. Democrats were not happy with Feingold.

"They were furious with me," Feingold said. "They said I was throwing away the seat because it wasn't my seat—which of course is true. But it wasn't their seat either. It's the seat of the people of Wisconsin." The party thought it had better political instincts than Feingold, who had taken the seat in an improbable victory in 1992. They thought they knew Wisconsin better than Feingold, who had lived there his entire life. They thought they could impose their will on him, as is often the case with inexperienced candidates or those depending on the party for financial assistance. But Feingold was neither inexperienced nor depending on the party for large amounts of money, and yet the heavy hand of the Democratic establishment in D.C. was bearing down on him.

Eventually, Feingold retained his seat, beating Neumann 50.8 to 48.7 percent. Since then, the maverick senator has voted against the Iraq War, was the lone vote against the Patriot Act, and his landmark campaign finance legislation (the McCain-Feingold bill) became law

in 2002. Despite votes like that—or perhaps because of them—
Feingold cruised to a comfortable 55-44 victory over Republican Tim
Michels in 2004.

The bull-in-a-china-shop approach of the Democratic establishment is felt with some regularity by Democratic candidates across the
country. It happened in Oklahoma where Feingold's media consultant, Milwaukee-based Steve Eichenbaum, pitched a potential job
to U.S. representative Brad Carson. A two-term congressman
looking for a promotion to the Senate, Carson saw the open seat as
the best possible chance in a state extremely hostile to Democrats in
federal races (Bush beat Al Gore 60-38 in 2000 and Republican senator Don Nickles beat his Democratic opponent, Don Carroll, 66-31
in 1998). Any Democrat running for statewide office in Oklahoma is
a serious underdog, and a "business as usual" campaign wasn't going
to win Carson the seat. Despite being one of the top-tier races for the
Senate in 2004, the campaign was one of the last to hire any media
firms, seeking an outside-the-box mix of consultants.

The longer Carson waited on hiring a media firm, the more nervous
and pushy the DSCC became and the more they upped the pressure.
At one point, using a standard D.C. ploy, party operatives tattled to
Chuck Todd, a political reporter at the beltway insider publication
The Hotline, that Carson wasn't being a good trooper. "Insiders are
extremely worried that Brad Carson is taking too active a role in his
own campaign, refusing to hire talented outsiders," Todd reported.
While the DSCC wanted Carson to hire inside-the-beltway consultants, Carson was keen on using Eichenbaum, a corporate advertising
executive who first created waves by helping Feingold win his dramatic 1992 upset victory using innovative, funny and clever ads, and
again helping Feingold win re-election in 1998.

Just as Carson was about to bring Eichenbaum on board, the DSCC
weighed in saying, "If that is what you're thinking, we need to talk,"
Carson told us when we caught up with him in Tulsa, Oklahoma, in

May 2005. Like any nonincumbent, Carson was dependent on the DSCC for millions of dollars and in no position to reject their advice. Carson ended up hiring the über-connected D.C. consulting firm of Murphy Putnam Media. (Steve Murphy ran Dick Gephardt's 2004 presidential campaign, among others.)

Things didn't go too smoothly. While he got along with Murphy, dealing with all the consultants from D.C. was an eye-opening experience for Carson. "That's the thing you'll learn about any consultant at the top level. They're above you in the food chain," said Carson. "You have to negotiate about what you do in your commercials. They call up the DSCC and complain if you're not doing the 'right thing.' They're a source of intelligence to people back in D.C. And these guys are all powerful people, prominent people. They aren't even working for you. It's an amazing thing in a lot of ways, really amazing." Carson lost the election 53-41 to Tom Coburn.

After his initial contact with Carson, Eichenbaum never heard back from the campaign and figured they just didn't see him as a good fit. When we went to Wisconsin and talked with him, he was rightly disturbed upon finding out that Carson was pressured to pick the other firm. "To find out that it was actually the party that told them that they couldn't use us after we ran a successful campaign for Feingold the last three times is really upsetting," Eichenbaum said. It wasn't the first run-in with the establishment for Eichenbaum, who was a key component of Feingold's "Miracle Campaign" in 1992. Feingold "ran against Democratic people that were pretty well entrenched in the party and the primary," recalls Eichenbaum. "One of them spent $3.1 million; the other one spent $4 million. We spent $220,000 and we got 70 percent of the vote. And those two other guys were so badly embarrassed and angry at us that the state Democratic Party people just locked us out."

You would think that scoring such an incredible upset would've been a rocket trip to the stars for the campaign consultants. But not for Eichenbaum. He serves mostly corporate clients and continues to do local political work and did Feingold's subsequent campaigns in 1998 and 2004, but any efforts to hire him got blocked by the Democratic establishment in D.C. Eichenbaum is not part of the D.C. consultant cocktail-party circuit. He's not one of *them*.

THE BELTWAY MAFIA

Unless there's a groundswell of opposition to business as usual, the Democratic Party's campaign machinery, with its ever-increasing inflow of money, will continue to function and lose as it has lately. The whole situation is one hell of a fix. The candidate needs money, but to get the money, he or she needs a strong connection to the party apparatus. And while the money the party raises for the candidate may vary by situation, the numbers can easily reach millions of dollars—a significant amount of the total spent by most campaigns. Those dollars, however, come with strings. The party wants assurances that the money is being spent wisely. It needs people in each campaign who will feed critical information from the inside. The consultants step in to fill that role.

Sometimes the party takes complete control of a campaign. Missouri state treasurer Nancy Farmer, who ran for the U.S. Senate in 2004, is a good example. A successful statewide candidate, Farmer had no real Democratic primary opposition and could take aim straight at the three-term Republican incumbent, Senator Christopher "Kit" Bond. The DSCC officials told her that they'd build her campaign and help her raise up to half of her campaign funds. Faced with an incumbent who was clearly going to raise three times as much, Farmer wasn't in the position to tell the party committee to leave her alone; that as state treasurer, she already knew how to win a statewide race in Missouri. So not only did the DSCC pick almost all the consultants for her campaign, they eventually forced significant changes in her campaign staff, including ousting her hand-picked campaign manager—the same one who had successfully managed Farmer's previous campaigns—in midstream and bringing in one of their own. Farmer lost to Bond by a 56-43 margin.

Journalist Amy Sullivan aired out some of the dirty laundry of the Democratic consultant world in "Fire the Consultants," an aptly titled exposé published in the January/February 2005 issue of *The Washington Monthly*. Among other things, she wrote that the DSCC and the Democratic Congressional Campaign Committee (DCCC) will officially say they don't foist their pet consultants on campaigns. But any candidate who is not independently wealthy and needs the party committee's money is likely to take its advice on consultants. "We needed the cash," one campaign veteran bluntly told Sullivan. "So of course, we were going to go with the consultants they recommended."

Feingold points to an alternative that can keep the party at bay: "If your support is based, as mine is, on 60,000 small contributors—the average contribution is $60—the party can *help* you, but they're not going to *own* you," he said.

Minnesota media maven Bill Hillsman, who was behind the first election in 1990 of Professor Paul Wellstone to the U.S. Senate and behind Jesse Ventura's quixotic (and victorious) 1998 campaign for Minnesota governor, told us that most D.C.-based consultants are more interested in keeping the party committee happy than in keeping the candidate happy. "Consultants should act as if they are working for their candidate, he's their client. Your loyalty should be to them," said Hillsman. "But that's not the case at all. Their loyalty, particularly true in congressional races, is to the DCCC because they care more about whether the DCCC is going to think they did a good job so they get more referrals, rather than whether their candidate actually wins."

This isn't meant to overstate the situation. The party organizations are not all-powerful machines. They are mostly involved with candidate selection, fundraising, and spending of those funds—mostly on media. But they do play a key role in staffing up campaigns, and that's where the cabal of media consultants and the party apparatus intersect—as consultants move effortlessly in and out of the party and various consulting gigs. And most candidates are inclined to play it "safe" when it comes to hiring a consultant. Paul Blank, Howard Dean's former political director, has seen this dynamic before. "Candidates think 'This is my one chance, my one campaign,' and the fear of going with somebody new or somebody untested in their one chance where they're going to spend the only money that they can ever afford to spend to run—that fear is what forces people to go with the status quo as opposed to going out on something a little more risky or something new." As they say in the business world, "No one ever got fired for buying IBM."

Instead of helping the new candidates by weeding out the incompetent consultants, the Democratic Party continues to thrust the same tired, old, unsuccessful consultants on new campaigns every cycle. And why not? Candidates come and go, their fate decided by voters, but inside D.C., the consultant class and the party officials move on to the next election and more business. It's a veritable revolving door—jobs abound, win or lose, as long as they are part of their clubby D.C. clique. Consider the case of Joe Hansen, a central character in Sullivan's news story. Hansen was employed by the DSCC at the same time that he was a partner in a direct-mail company. Hansen, who worked at the DSCC from 1998 to 2002 (first as executive director, then as field director) would begin working closely with candidates early in the campaign. Soon, he would arrange for his company to provide direct-mail services for the candidate. Since he was their liaison to the DSCC (and the campaign contributions that came through the DSCC), the candidates wanted Hansen on their side. What better way than hiring Hansen's company to do their direct mail? Inside the beltway, such conflicts of interest are ignored with a wink and a nod.

Look through any of the party committees' filings and you'll find consultant after consultant on the payroll holding official party committee positions, blurring the line between employees and consultants. And if you look deep enough, you'll find that those same consultants are partners in firms that provide services to the candidates' campaigns. Joe Hansen isn't alone. There are more like him at the DSCC, the DCCC, and the DNC.

Call it a cash cow, an incestuous circle, or an "old boy asshole network" (as one hardened political campaigner described it to us), the point is, there is no accountability and the system rewards networking and schmoozing skills in D.C., not performance and results in elections. It only continues because those that benefit from this system work to protect their racket from those wishing to expose it.

And no one wants to talk publicly about these ugly insider problems. "In general, a Mafia-like code of omerta operates," wrote Sullivan. "Few insiders dare complain about the hammerlock loser consultants have on the process—certainly neither the professional campaign operatives whom the consultants hire nor the journalists to whom the consultants feed juicy inside-the-room detail."

Journalist and blogger Marc Ambinder wrote a scathing article for the D.C. insider publication *Hotline* on December 21, 2005, that exposed "an open secret in Washington that many big-name, partisan political strategy firms have affiliates that handle non-partisan, revenue-producing corporate accounts" (such as PhRMA, the lobby of the pharmaceutical industry handled in McMahon's media firm by partner John Donovan) that work against progressive interests. Afterwards, Ambinder relayed to us, "Writing about consultants can be hard for political reporters because they're often our best sources. That said, the groves of the political consulting world are fertile with juicy stories." It's an acknowledgement of the powerful role that consultants have, and there are too few Sullivans and Ambinders who write about the D.C. feast, and even fewer political professionals who will talk about it on the record.

One of the few who *will* talk is veteran political strategist Mike Ford, who mentored Howard Dean's unconventional campaign manager Joe Trippi and has worked a number of presidential campaigns with his wife Sally Ford. And not only did he talk, he minced no words. "It's a nasty, bullshit business, consulting," Mike Ford told us when we met up with the couple in Baltimore in June 2005. Sally Ford added, "It's also become a very lucrative business." There's nothing wrong with having the tough work of political consulting be lucrative, especially if it draws the best and brightest to the business and leads to electoral victories. But the system is not a meritocracy— it rewards too many losers and keeps too many talented people out.

"Consultants haven't been very good for the Democratic Party," Mike Ford said. "You'll have a consultant who will go after potential candidates and flat out lie to them. They will say, 'Oh yeah, you've got a chance, you've got to run.' And they have no chance in the world!" Ford offers the case of Bob Shrum, the man who had lost seven presidential elections and won zero when hired by Kerry in 2004, which has now made Shrum's win-loss record 0-8. In between, Shrum handled dozens of other campaigns in a career that began as a speechwriter, his most famous being Ted Kennedy's "The dream shall never die" concession speech at the 1980 Democratic national convention. "Bob Shrum is the classic case," said Ford. "Shrum came into politics in a very admirable way, as a speechwriter. He was eloquent and then became a sort of businessman and you can judge the quality of his work. But here's my point—look up Al Checchi."

Al Checchi, the multimillionaire head of Northwest Airlines, decided to run for governor of California in 1998. A first-time candidate, Checchi wanted the most experienced consultants and ended up hiring the most expensive ones like Clinton pollster Mark Penn—and

Shrum. Checchi went down in defeat with a pitiful 13 percent of the primary vote losing to U.S. representative Jane Harman and Lieutenant Governor Gray Davis (who went on to become governor, beating Republican Dan Lungren in the general election). The businessman candidate, Checchi spent over $40 million in the losing cause. Syndicated columnist and blogger Arianna Huffington estimated that Penn and Shrum made out with $2 million each for running Checchi into the ground.[33] (And that doesn't include income Shrum earned from other campaigns he was handling that same election cycle, including John Edwards' first senatorial run in North Carolina.)

Said Ford: "I know Al Checchi, we went to grade school and we played ball together and were friends. Checchi got ripped off by Shrum. I watched this in horror. Look at how much of his own money Shrum had him spend to come in third out of three."

It might seem easy to brush aside the Shrum-Checchi case as an exception, but sadly it's more the rule, especially for campaigns with deep pockets. As Sullivan notes: "One of the most obvious and least discussed reasons Democrats continue to lose is the consultants. Every sports fan knows that if a team boasts a losing record several seasons in a row, the coach has to be replaced with someone who can win. Yet when it comes to political consultants, Democrats seem incapable of taking this basic managerial step."

Dean Rindy is a Texas consultant who has worked state and congressional contests for over a decade. From his vantage point, he sees the basic problem of the D.C. establishment as one of isolation, of operating in a bubble. "There are hacks, there are opportunists, and the greatest problem inside the beltway isn't a lack of intelligence—it's the fact that when you only talk to the people you know it becomes very intellectually incestuous," Rindy said. "It produces a conventional wisdom and a common consensus that often runs well behind what's happening in the rest of the country."

To make matters worse, these insiders aren't necessarily playing to win. A firm in D.C. racks up a serious (and lucrative) client list by traveling the safe insider path. The system provides no incentives for successful risk taking or finding innovative ways to win. Instead, when a consultant finds something that works once, he or she keeps on selling the same thing to as many clients as possible. Eichenbaum, Feingold's adman, describes their motivation. "Nobody wants to win. That isn't their main objective. Their main objective is, 'I don't want to get fired. So I'm going to make every decision so that if it doesn't work out, it can never come back and kick me in the ass and get me fired.' And that is a shitty way to do business," he says. "It's a shitty way to do advertising and I see that everywhere. I see the Democratic Party doing that on every single level, every single thing they do, every policy they make. Every time they choose not to speak out on issues they ought to be speaking out on is because they're covering their ass.

"Nobody does anything anymore on the basis of what's right, or to try to break through, or to try to do something different. It's just all about, 'God, just don't let me get fired.' And as long as this country runs that way on everything, we're going to get our ass kicked, whether it's cars, or politicians, it doesn't matter what it is."

The campaigns, the candidates, and the growing number of small donors deserve accountability. Yet none currently exists. After the elections are over, losing candidates disappear and are forgotten, while the consultants hustle for new business no matter what their win-loss record. And given that over 50 percent of a campaign's budget is spent on media, nothing makes the case for reform more obvious than the commissions paid to the all-powerful media consultants.

THE COMMISSION RACKET

Media expenditures are a serious business. While most campaign consultants and staffers earn a set salary or perhaps a retainer, media consultants get to gorge on commissions of 7 to 15 percent of every ad dollar spent by a campaign. Those percentages can reach into millions of dollars for competitive congressional races and top-of-the-ballot races, all for whipping out sixty-second spots, running them by focus groups, and then placing the ads. Good ads or bad, win or lose, the commissions roll in.

It's a compensation model that most sophisticated advertisers in the corporate sector abandoned ten to twenty years ago. According to Joe Cappo, author of *The Future of Advertising*, about 90 percent of today's product advertising is free of commission, while about 90 percent of the political world continues to embrace it. This is perhaps one of the most obvious conflicts of interest that a media consultant faces. Unlike the business world, campaign media consultants advise the candidates about how much TV ad time to buy; generally, the rule of thumb is to buy as much as they can afford. It's a particularly obscene amount of compensation when we consider that in most campaigns, hundreds of volunteers work for free and staffers work full-time for as little as $500 a month.

The 2004 presidential campaign was the gravy train for well-connected political consultants, led by Shrum. Using a shell company called Riverfront Media, a group of entrenched media consultants managed $150 million in advertising for Kerry and the DNC, earning $11 million in commissions (about 7 percent). According to the *Washington Post*, Shrum's firm (Shrum, Devine & Donilon) took $5 million from the Riverfront Media pot along with $3 million in payments for other undisclosed services from the Kerry campaign.[34]

Nancy Todd Tyner, president of the American Association of Political Consultants, tried to shrug off the situation: "If you want to get the best media consultant, this is the way it's done."[35] That's not how George W. Bush did it. His campaign paid their media consultants a flat fee of $6 million and saved themselves a whopping $8 million compared to what Kerry and the Democrats spent. And to make the fee disparity that much starker, the RNC and Bush campaigns collectively placed $222 million worth of ads compared to the DNC and Kerry campaign's $150 million.

In response to criticisms about commission-based compensation models, media consultants argue that doing away with commissions would hurt challenger candidates, as they are the ones without a lot of money (especially at the beginning of a campaign). In such an arrangement, the ad consultant comes on without pay, with the understanding that if the candidate's campaign takes off, the media consultant will be well compensated through the commissions. It's similar to personal injury lawyers who take plaintiffs' cases on a contingency basis and collect a percentage of the award if they win. In a campaign, the media consultant assumes the risk of no payoff versus big payoff. This is a legitimate defense of commissions, and one that particularly applies to small-budget campaigns. But certainly, for the top thirty House races and top ten Senate races every election year, there isn't much question whether there will be millions spent on advertising. At the least, candidates should feel free to negotiate the terms.

Brad Carson was able to negotiate a $250,000 flat fee for his Senate race in 2004. Democratic senator Hillary Clinton of New York negotiated a fee with media consultant Mandy Grunwald for her 2000 race. Consultants like Steve Eichenbaum and Bill Hillsman are willing to work for flat fees and retainers rather than commissions. It can be done, and should be done at the Senate and presidential level.

Commission-based advertising provides the wrong kind of incentives, where frequency trumps quality. "If media is your biggest line item and you're trying to save money on media, doesn't it make sense that if somebody actually paid attention to the commercial the first time and liked it and was involved in it and actually absorbed the information the first time, then you can run less media?" asks Hillsman, who has been a thorn in the side of the consulting establishment for years. "You don't have to get these frequency levels of eight or nine or ten with a good commercial." This makes sense, but not for consultants working on commission, wanting huge ad expenditures to pad their bottom line.

OLD ADS, NEW AGE

There is a belief in Washington, particularly among Democratic media firms producing television advertising, that selling candidates is very different from selling consumer products. You've seen the political ads and the laundry list of items squeezed into those thirty-second spots—the millions proposed for health care and education, the millions to be saved from deficit reduction, and so on. Steve McMahon, who was Howard Dean's media consultant in the 2004 election cycle, told Ryan Lizza of *New York* magazine in April 2003 that consumer-product ads have a different purpose altogether from political campaign ads: "The advertising they produce is meant to communicate an emotion or feeling, and what we do is move public opinion."[36]

With this sort of mentality, it's understandable why McMahon delivered the infamous ad of Dean during the crucial last week of the Iowa caucuses. The ad had Dean standing in front of a white background saying, "This election is about power. About who runs the country and who owns it." The ad, copying spots done by Errol Morris for Apple's Macintosh computers that used ordinary people giving testimonials, was a loser from the get-go. Jerome, who was at the Dean campaign headquarters in Vermont while the campaign was collapsing, mentioned the criticism of the ads to McMahon. He wisecracked: "When the candidate loses, they say the ads were crappy, and when the candidate wins, they say the ads were terrific." It's worth reading that statement again. What it really says is that the media guys are never wrong.

No self-respecting marketing firm would ever replicate that emotionless white background for their corporate clients. Pepsi doesn't run ads with a guy standing in front of a white background saying, "Drink this, it's good. Really." And those Apple commercials the Dean ad was trying to emulate? They were lifestyle- and brand-building ads. As Dean's campaign manager Joe Trippi (who didn't produce any of the Dean TV spots) was quoted in Roger Simon's piece in *U.S. News and World Report* in July 2004: "Everyone agrees the last spot could have been better."

For Democratic candidates, their problem is that the media consultants and agencies don't know if their ads will work or not until *after* they've already spent hundreds of thousands or millions of dollars airing the ad. There is no testing done to determine how people will respond to an ad *before* they spend the money to buy airtime.

We learned about this issue visiting Joan Blades and Wes Boyd, the cofounders of MoveOn.org, at their Berkeley, California, bungalow. Blades and Boyd ran millions of dollars of issue ads nationwide attacking George Bush during the 2004 political season, especially in battleground states. Before airing their ads they made a concerted effort to see if they would be effective. They would run their test spot in a small market, and not run it in another. They would poll both markets before and after the spots ran. Then they would compare numbers to see if their ad had any effect. While not a perfect system, it was a simple process for providing at least some measurement for an ad's success (or lack thereof).

"We used Stan Greenberg [CEO of Greenberg Quinlan Rosner Research]," said Boyd. "I really had to push this. This is not something that is done in Washington as far as we can tell. What they do is 'focus group.' When they say something's tested they do focus groups. And focus groups are just like group dynamics—who knows, you can learn a little bit from them, but in terms of really knowing what the big dynamics are, it's kind of useless." We asked around, and though media consultants vowed they did occasionally market test spots, the barrier was time.

For political consultants, it's all busywork they'd rather avoid doing or learning how to do. "Consultants really don't want this kind of testing because of accountability," Boyd said. "Why would consultants want testing that might show that their ad was crap? They don't, and so they don't do it, and their clients don't demand it."

In the last ten or twenty years, political consulting firms in Washington, D.C., have become the sole specialists in political advertising as Stuart Elliott, a media critic at the *New York Times*, told us over snacks in the *Times* cafeteria. "Occasionally, on the federal level, you might have a blue ribbon panel of professional advertising executives appointed by a presidential candidate to consult. And then once in a great while, like with Reagan in 1984, or Clinton in 1992, you might have some of the ideas they contribute actually make it on the air in the form of TV commercials," Elliott said. "But for the most part, these specialty firms create the political advertising, and that's why political advertising is so calcified into the sort of mode that it's been in for all these years, and not moved forward the way traditional product advertising has."

One such calcified notion is that viewers respond differently to political commercials than they do to product commercials. Persuasion, not emotion, as McMahon would say. Tell that to the Republicans. Here is what Lizza reported in his *New York* magazine piece: "[Bush ad maker Stuart] Stevens looks at the gap between Washington political firms that practice the art of issue-oriented persuasion and New York ad firms that specialize in triggering emotions, and he sees lessons to be learned. 'I can convince you better than someone from Madison Avenue that eating hamburgers at Burger King gives you cancer,' he says. 'But they are making you feel emotional and involved in eating hamburgers. That's pretty impressive. I think people who can make you feel emotionally involved about eating hamburgers have something to teach you about defending the country or improving education.'"

Steve Eichenbaum, whose clients come mostly from the corporate world, absolutely rejects the notion that political and corporate ads are different. "People somehow want to believe that we treat political candidates different than we do a box of cereal, but the truth of the matter is there's really more similarities than there are differences," he said. The biggest similarity? "For both political and product ads, people feel that they are being manipulated. So if people automatically mistrust facts and numbers, how do you reach them? By pulling emotional chords. By making people feel good about the candidate, not convincing them that her legislative priorities are better than her opponent's."

In the 2002 gubernatorial race in Florida, Democrat Bill McBride ran the typical Democratic ads—lists of the things going wrong in Florida, and how he would fix them. The ads were replete with dollar signs and details, which his media consultant hoped, would prove the candidate's commitment to the various issues. On the other side, incumbent governor Jeb Bush's ad team hit with powerful emotional ads. Take for example this highly effective ad targeting the Latino community, titled "Banderas" (Flags).[37] A succession of flags—Cuban, Mexican, Colombian, Dominican, Venezuelan, Nicaraguan—flutter on camera, full screen, and finally the flag of the state of Florida.

NARRATOR (in Spanish):
It doesn't matter where we come from
Or why we come
We have found opportunity in this land
A better education for our children
The health care our families deserve
A state that has opened up its heart
And has told us, "This is our home"

JEB BUSH (speaking to the camera in perfect Spanish):

We all want a better life

Together, we're making this all possible in this land

Our home (*Nuestro hogar*)

Florida

Our house (*Nuestra casa*)

It's impossible to be a Latin American immigrant and watch that ad without getting goose bumps. Sergio Bendixen, a Miami-based Democratic media consultant specializing in Spanish-language advertising, couldn't rave enough about the ad. "The narration of 'Banderas' connected emotionally with Latin American immigrants by recognizing the nationalistic feelings they still have for their country of origin, even though they are now committed to a life in the United States." But some Democrats were in denial. A Florida Democratic Party spokesman was dismissive of the "Banderas" ad, telling the *Puerto Rico Herald* that "No amount of marketing will change that Jeb Bush is wrong on the issues."[38] But not only did Bush cruise to reelection, he won a solid majority of the state's estimated one million Hispanics. And not just a majority of Cubans, who overwhelmingly vote Republican and gave Jeb 80 percent of their vote, but Democratic-leaning non-Cubans as well, 55 percent of whom voted for Bush.

In two separate polls of the 2004 election (Public Opinion Strategy and Fabrizio), the top three ads remembered most by viewers were all done by Republicans or their aligned groups—"Ashley," "Swift Boat," and "Wolves." "Ashley" was aired by Progress for America Voter Fund (a 527 group), and showed Bush hugging the Ohio girl named Ashley, whose mother was killed in the 9/11 attacks, while the woman's father stated, "What I saw was what I want to see in the heart and in the soul of the man who sits in the highest-elected office in our country." The "Swift Boat Veterans for Truth" was a 527 group that aired a variety of attack ads, basically claiming that John Kerry lied about his war record. "Wolves" was an ad aired late in 2004 by the Bush-Cheney campaign, which showed a pack of wolves circling in, while the narrator implied that Kerry would vote against military spending. All three were nonconventional ads that visually and rhetorically pulled emotional strings rather than attempted to persuade voters with facts and hard information. Mark Mellman, who was John Kerry's pollster for the 2004 presidential election, acknowledges that these ads are the most memorable, but categorically states "all the research suggests there's absolutely no correlation between the memorability of an ad, on the one hand, and its persuasiveness, on the other . . . there is no correlation . . . the fact that an ad is memorable does not mean it's persuasive. There is a difference. Don't ask me. Walk down the street to the business school people. They'll tell you that."[39]

Bill Hillsman scoffs at the implication that persuasion is the end-all indicator for a successful political ad. "Memorability, as well as persuadability, is one of the key matrices of testing advertising effectiveness. To argue otherwise not only defies common sense, it's the kind of idiocy that has made the Democratic Party the persuasive power it is today," he said. "You don't have to go to a business school to find that out. Walk down the street to the nearest merchant. They'll tell you that." But speaking on behalf of those forgettable TV ads done for Kerry, Mellman said, "There really isn't a relationship between memorability and persuasion. We are not in the business of creating ads that were going to be memorable."

Robyn McIver, global planning director at Ogilvy Public Relations Worldwide, points to research that contradicts Mellman. "According to the research firm Millward Brown, memorability and persuasiveness are two different measures that can work independently of each other. In their advertising effectiveness measurement tool, the scores are separate and you must have both to have an ad that works," she explained to us in July 2005 over coffee in New York City, and then offered an example. "We recently tested an ad where a giant salmon swallows a bear. That event, while highly memorable, wasn't persuasive. Persuasive scores are generated by telling people something they do not know that is relevant. For example, 'John Kerry voted to raise taxes fifty times' is not memorable to anyone because all Democrats do this. However, 'John Kerry lied about his war record' could be both memorable and persuasive. Persuasive because it's news to someone and memorable because it relates to his character and is an unusual claim."

The "Swift Boat Veterans for Truth" ads were absolutely memorable—and effective. Those ads featured Vietnam War veterans criticizing John Kerry for supposedly lying about his medals and war record. Steve Rosenthal, president of the now-defunct 527 organization America Coming Together (ACT), noted that post-2004 focus groups in Ohio found voters "who not only remembered the ads, chapter and verse, having seen them or not, but would recite directly from the ads and say, 'How could I vote for John Kerry when people who served with him—which wasn't the case, by the way—didn't think he was fit to be commander-in-chief?' So they were extremely effective ads." But "no correlation" say the media and polling consultants on the Democratic side.

In Virginia's 2005 gubernatorial race, Republican media consultant Scott Howell created what quickly became know as the "Hitler Ad" because of a line about the Democratic candidate saying "Tim Kaine says that Adolf Hitler doesn't qualify for the death penalty." The emotional impact of the ad, which used a father of a murder victim to attack Kaine over his opposition to the death penalty, was stark. "Emotion, whether it's humor, angst, whether it makes you laugh or cry, it helps people to respond," Howell told *The Nation*.[40] "We're in a sound-bite world, and you have to work to get people's attention." Ads like that are clearly below-the-belt hits and few would argue that the Democrats should sink that low. But Democrats and their ad makers ought to accept the reality that tugging at people's hearts, not just their heads, produces results.

Sometimes it's the little things that create the memorable connection. Like in 2004, when the Republicans hired Hal Riney, who did voiceovers for the original Miller Beer, and has the macho 1950s blue-collar voice that is so familiar to many Americans. Miller beer probably had a $180 million ad campaign, Hillsman estimated, and "that voice was in a lot of minds already. And he's in exactly that demographic that the Republicans really wanted—talking to blue-collar guys, and it really worked for them."

The strong backlash in Virginia against the Hitler ad (two of three Virginia voters said the ads were "unfair," including nearly 75 percent of the self-described independents[41]) showed that it's a gamble to toy with people's emotions. And as we've noted, Democratic consultants are not the type to take these sorts of gambles. An edgy ad may propel a candidate to victory or lead to a campaign implosion. But where does that leave the Democrats—always waiting to see whether the Republican media consultants like Howell can drive the emotional wedge in the campaign to victory, or fail? The effectiveness of Howell, who won eleven of twelve contests in 2002, speaks for itself. Even Kaine's Democratic media strategists, David Eichenbaum (no relation to Steve Eichenbaum) and Karl Struble, who the *Washington Post* says "knew the television attack was coming, but they didn't know what form it would take," seem to be at the mercy of the Republicans' use of emotion in ads.[42]

In addition, only Republicans regularly reach out to Madison Avenue for help in their party's advertising efforts. Some of the most creative material in Republican political campaigns has come out of corporate advertising shops. For instance, longtime BBDO chairman Phil Dusenberry, who came up with "We bring good things to life" ads for GE, and the "Pepsi Generation" idea for Pepsi, also helped create (with Hal Riney and other Madison Avenue all-stars) Reagan's "Morning in America" ads. That was 1984. In 2004, Stuart Stevens, who came out of Republican politics, and Madison

Avenue's Harold Kaplan and Vada Hill, advised the Bush ad makers alongside an informal group of other New Yorkers in the ad business.

In fact, Republicans have been using media professionals since Dwight Eisenhower, when adman Rosser Reeves, from the Ted Bates ad agency, sold Eisenhower on the idea of running television ads ahead of *I Love Lucy*. The *Times'* Elliott recalls the innovation of the Eisenhower team. "What they did was shoot Eisenhower in a room addressing what we call sound bites now, little pat answers about issues of the day, and then after that they went out and filmed people on the streets of New York asking the questions," he explained. "That was how all this subterfuge that they're still doing was born. They had the answers first and then they got people to ask the questions. Then they edited it in the opposite way, put those on the air, and of course they helped Eisenhower beat the pants off of Adlai Stevenson."

From that effective use of television ads sprung the media-political advertising consultant. And with the growth of the political campaigning industry, the creation of political ads shifted from New York to Washington, D.C. And there the profession has been stuck ever since, content to collect commissions and stagnating in its old-fashioned approach to political advertising.

The key to effective advertising for Democrats is not only to get beyond the corrupt commission model of media saturation, but also to find more creative ways to reach the audience that is watching less and less broadcast television and getting its news and entertainment more and more from new media. The next challenge in campaign messaging is to stay ahead of the curve when it comes to using new media to target specific audiences with the messages that will resonate with them. In this area, too, the Democrats need to shed the old ways and embrace the new.

THE CHANGING MEDIA LANDSCAPE

The ways Americans receive their news and entertainment is shifting fast. Satellite and cable television carry hundreds of stations, fragmenting the TV audience. Internet-based media continue to grow at astonishing rates and in directions few could have foreseen even a few years ago. Satellite radio is stealing listeners from local broadcast stations. Video games now regularly outperform the most successful movies, and have development budgets that rival the biggest Hollywood blockbusters. TiVo and other digital recorders allow viewers to watch their favorite programs when they want and without those pesky commercials.

Meanwhile, TV advertising as a percentage of total product advertising is plunging. Despite that, the inept media consultants driving John Kerry's 2004 strategy acted as if it were still 1984. In a conference call with bloggers and other members of the political media one night during the last week of the campaign, Tad Devine, a partner with Shrum in the media-consulting agency of Shrum, Devine & Donilon, triumphantly boasted that Kerry was running 15 to 25 percent more TV commercials than Bush in Florida in that critical final week of the race. The Kerry campaign had hoarded its cash for this final push, and Devine confidently talked about "dominating" the airwaves that last week. Shrum, Devine & Donilon mistakenly thought that saturation—ten Kerry ads for every eight Bush ads viewed by the average Florida TV viewer—would assure a Kerry victory. They were waging a 1980s-era media campaign.

In the early 1970s, advertisers could reach 90 percent of households during prime time on the three major networks. Today, the three major networks and the Fox Network capture less than 40 percent.[43] According to the New Politics Institute,* there are fundamental

*Markos is a founding fellow of the New Politics Institute, run by NDN's Simon Rosenberg.

shifts happening within the U.S. media and advertising industries that campaigns would be foolish to ignore.[44] Product advertisers are shifting ad dollars away from broadcast television's 6 major networks into the diffused market of the 390 cable television networks, which now exceed broadcast networks in aggregate viewers. During the 1980s, most people, even with cable, had about twenty channels, whereas now hundreds of channels are offered. The popularity of satellite radio is busting open the radio networks. And then there's the internet. In 2005, 168 million people in the United States were using the internet at home, work, or at school.[45] The percentage of those with internet access will grow from 66 percent in 2003, to 79 percent in 2008. By 2008, half of the online population will have broadband high-speed internet access.[46]

The view that saturation on broadcast TV equals reach—expressed by Devine and by other Democratic media consultants—is a 1980s notion that no longer holds true. Today, reach requires moving beyond saturation-level television network buys, to smaller, targeted buys on cable networks, across radio, and of course, online. Republicans already realize the landscape has shifted, and in the last election cycle their aggressive adaptation to the new media paid dividends. Rather than spend nearly all their money targeting undecided voters and nonvoters via network television saturation, the Bush campaign funneled millions into precisely targeted cable-television and talk-radio outlets.

Ken Mehlman, campaign manager for Bush-Cheney in 2004, summed it up following Bush's win. "The traditional buying ads on three channels, doing some robo calls, and doing some paid mail as a voter contact program is insufficient."[47] But that pretty much sums up what Kerry's media consultants relied upon.

Devine, in a meeting of the presidential campaign consultants at Harvard following the 2004 election, clarified the "fundamental difference" between the two campaigns as one of strategic orientation. Referring to the notion that the handful of battleground states was all that mattered, Devine stated: "That's where we sent our most precious resource—our candidates. That's where we spent our money on television. We did not have national cable buys. We did not do national radio buys. We approached the election differently." Mehlman, who was also at the event, said the Republican strategy involved a multifaceted approach "that reached people not just on the networks but increasingly on cable, increasingly on radio, increasingly in different venues."[48]

ACT's Steve Rosenthal believes it was this effort by Republicans that pushed them over the top. He also believes that the way Republicans drove their vote up wasn't necessarily through organization, but "was largely through message, with an excellent campaign buying cable TV and radio, getting local newspaper ads, and a very local campaign." Democrats ran a terrific ground effort, but got beat because the Republicans more effectively got their message to their supporters.[49]

Glenn Smith, a long-term Democratic consultant in Texas who describes himself as "recovered" and "born-again" after leaving the business, told us in Austin in July 2005, "As television is less and less important, it's going to take the money out of this. And when you take the money out of it, that's going to help break up the consortium."

The challenge for campaign consultants is to move beyond television. This means reaching target audiences on the internet, radio, and over direct mail. But beyond that, campaigns need to create information databases on voters and engage in sophisticated targeting of the message based on creating voter profiles. The campaigns that win the tough races in the future are going to be those that move beyond the world of showing repetitive television ads, to the brave new digital world we already live in—in which terms like "microtargeting," "market segmentation," and "data mining" abound.

INFORMATION-AGE CAMPAIGNS

Mike McCurry, the former Bill Clinton spokesman and a consultant for Kerry in 2004, gave the most succinct postmortem of the 2004 presidential campaign: "We ran the last best campaign of the twentieth century. Republicans began what it takes to run campaigns in the twenty-first century."

Up until 2000, Democrats could always rely upon their superior "get out the vote" (GOTV) operation to squeeze more votes from the base on election day than Republicans. The year 1994—when Republican GOTV efforts exceeded Democratic efforts—was seen as an aberration. In reality, it was a sign of things to come. Republicans have since fine-tuned their GOTV machine to the point that in 2002 and 2004 they clearly won the GOTV war. With no primary battle to worry about, Bush and his Republican team were able to focus time and money on field tests of their new ground strategy in the 2002 and 2004 elections, finance advanced research that merged voter databases with polling information, and effectively engage their supporters to turn out on election day.

After $50 million in testing and research, the GOP rolled out its "72-Hour Effort" in 2002, focusing on election day and the two preceding days. They targeted voters with calls, flyers, and door-to-door visits—the same way Democrats do. But while Democratic-aligned groups concentrated heavily in Democratic areas (ACT targeted districts that had over 70 percent "Democratic performance"), Republicans took it to the next level, competing everywhere, including those very same 70 percent "Democratic performance" districts.

And new database technology, along with some creativity, made it all possible.

Building a national database of voters is relatively new to politics. Hal Malchow, author of *The New Political Targeting*, believes that it's time that campaigns adopt the available technology. The growth and improvement in accuracy of voter lists over the past couple of decades has created a political industry of companies that build voter files. Almost all counties have computerized their voter lists, and many states have made their lists available at inexpensive rates.

Available data can be used to identify the strength and trend of the party vote down to the precinct level. Parties and campaigns can then purchase census data, adding things such as income, ethnicity, and education level to the voter list. And finally, there is the data used in commercial direct marketing, which can also be a powerful targeting tool. Called "narrow-casting" or "micro-targeting," Republican campaigns can use that information to target, say, urban gun owners that have been voting Democratic; or Democrats can target a message about stem-cell research to Republicans that have family members with Alzheimer's or Parkinson's disease. It's a treasure trove of data that's available for the taking by campaigns, both through direct mail and, increasingly, over the internet. But, according to Malchow, all too few campaigns make good use of it.

The Bush campaign and the Republican National Committee (RNC) aggressively combined consumer information with voter file data. They gained knowledge of what television shows their supporters watched, the magazines they read, even their choice of beverage. The Democrats had access to the same sort of information, through a database at DNC headquarters dubbed the "DataMart," that merged the consumer census data information with voter identification, but this wasn't used effectively by the Kerry campaign, which ignored predominantly Republican areas.

According to a December 30, 2004, *Washington Post* story by Thomas Edsall and James Grimaldi, the Bush campaign's new ground operation was able to identify potential voters four times more accurately than through traditional direct mail, phone banks, and door-to-door canvassing. As for the Democrats, the story quoted one party operative who helped the DNC coordinate voter contact: "Very few people understand how much work it takes to get this technology to actually produce political results. We are one election cycle behind them in this area."

Terry McAuliffe, the DNC Chairman at the time, told the *Post* reporters that the Republicans "were smart. They came into our neighborhoods. They came into Democratic areas with very specific targeted messages to take Democratic voters away from us. They were much more sophisticated in their message delivery."

Perhaps the biggest difference between the way Democrats and Republicans communicated with voters, besides the more sophisticated use of technology and data, was that the Republicans have been targeting *all* voters—Republicans, Democrats, independents—and doing it all year long, not just in the last weeks of an election. In the heat of a campaign, Republicans were content to let dueling Democratic and Republican TV ads cancel each other out. The money on both sides was essentially wasted, and the GOP was just fine with that. But in direct mail, as McAuliffe grudgingly admitted, the Republicans were targeting Independents and Democrats, not just Republicans.

And that strategy paid off in a big way. While the Democratic ground operation increased turnout and Kerry's vote by 6.8 million votes over Gore in 2000, the Republican strategy increased their turnout and Bush's vote by nearly 10.5 million votes compared to 2000. Although the DNC was ready to do cluster targeting across the entire voter landscape in 2004 according to a senior official, the Kerry campaign decided to stick with turning out the Democratic base and persuading independents, leaving predominantly Republican areas alone to hear only one side of the story.

Outside the party structure, some 527 groups have begun to find new ways to reach voters using new technological tools. Besides ACT, which used paid staffers in battleground states to go door-to-door gathering information for micro-targeting of voters, another group that made good use of individualized voter outreach was Women's Voices. Women Vote (WVWV). They ran successful programs in eighteen states to register and turn out unmarried women voters, one of the most important, but underutilized progressive constituency groups for Democrats. WVWV built their battleground list of twenty-one million unmarried women, then targeted them with direct mail, phone calls, and television advertising, while testing the effectiveness of their efforts against control groups.

Another area where Democrats need to ramp up their efforts is in polling. Traditionally, D.C. pollsters will provide simple "crosstab" polling—ask a bunch of people a question, then divide the answers by several demographic categories like sex, age, political affiliation, geography, and education. But the research must be deeper and go beyond mere compilation of a database of voter records and consumer information. Demographics are taking a backseat to lifestyle groupings in predicting voter trends, and have less predictive value in determining a voter's ideology than what cable channels they watch, what magazines they read, what cars they drive, what websites they visit, and so on. What a person believes matters more than whatever social group that person belongs to, and is a much stronger predictor of party affiliation. What's more important is not who you are, demographically speaking, but what you believe. Yet traditional polling, which still dominates the political world, continues to focus on demographics, depriving campaigns of critical data that would allow "narrow-casting" of tailored message to voters based on their identity.

Called "psychographics" or values-based research, the practice has been used regularly among the private sector to fine-tune marketing campaigns. "Psychographic analyses for Schlitz beer, for example, revealed that heavy beer drinkers were real macho men who feel that pleasures in their lives are few and far between, and they want something more, according to Joseph Plummer, the researcher who conducted the study," explained the March 1988 edition of *Psychology*

Today. "This insight led to Schlitz commercials that told people 'You only go around once,' so you might as well 'reach for all the gusto you can.'" One more example: A-1 Steak Sauce is used predominantly on hamburger meat. But marketing it as a steak product helps sell it to the primary market—low-income people who feel "upscale" by putting it in their shopping carts.

This sort of research is nearly nonexistent in Democratic circles, especially inside the beltway. Joel Wright, who has done over fifteen ballot measures and initiatives in Arizona over the past twenty years, is a rare exception. Wright told us, up in the Arizona mountains where he lives, that "Republicans are successfully moving into this area of voter targeting and contact-based on political decision making. They are blending values and psychological measurements with demographics to build a comprehensive, deep and multidimensional picture of voters. That allows them to understand and reach deep psychological and values dynamics and hot buttons, which simplify decision making for voters. In my view, Republicans are focused on talking to people, human beings, while Democrats continue to talk to categories and characteristics."

Wright added, "And on the Democratic side, this works fine for the gravy train beltway pollsters. The work is quick, easy for them. And lucrative." Wright scoffs at the conventional wisdom that polling is only a "snapshot" of the electorate, a moment frozen in time. "The snapshot concept means that polling has a limited shelf life, it gets old, 'yellowed,' out of date," he says. "So, Ms. Candidate must have her beltway pollster blow in, provide a simple crosstab update, who then mails the bill and blows town for his or her next client. This happens repeatedly over the course of a campaign. Values, psychology and the meanings voters internalize over a lifetime on political concerns do not change dramatically over short periods of time, particularly a twelve-to-eighteen-month campaign. The idea of a snapshot actually means more jobs, more billing, more production for the pollster." Just like the media consultants, there are less than a dozen Democratic polling firms that do the lion's share of the party's top races each cycle. And similarly, the pollsters' cartel is rewarded for longevity and connections, rather than innovation and results.

THE COST OF FAILURE

After each Democratic loss, the party's resident apologists have trotted out the same tired excuse—Republicans outspent us! That used to be true, but no longer. Democrats achieved financial parity with the Republicans for the first time in 2004, in large part because of donations from internet-based rabble-rousers, ending that lame excuse.[50]

The small donors gave the Democratic Party more money than ever, the consultants got rich while spending more money than ever, and we still lost. As Dan Balz reported in the *Washington Post* on February 19, 2005: "Figures compiled by the Center for Responsive Politics show that in 2003 and 2004, the DNC raised $171 million in contributions of less than $250. That represented 42 percent of the $404.5 million raised from all sources by the committee. Four years ago, before large soft-money contributions were banned by the new campaign finance reform law, the DNC raised a total of $260 million from all sources. Kerry's campaign raised an additional $84 million in contributions under $250."

The party has survived the soft-money ban because small donors stepped up to the plate, but a large chunk of the new small donors are unlikely to continue their donations if the Democrats keep losing elections and if there is no accountability for the consultants and for the Democratic Party committees.

Besides accountability, it is just plain ugly to see fat-cat consultants walk away with millions of dollars while millions of small donors are scraping up enough cash to send in their $50 donation. Message forums on sites like Daily Kos, MyDD, Eschaton, Democratic Underground, Blog for America, and others were full of testimonials from people with few resources sacrificing what they could for the cause. One commenter on Daily Kos wrote of skipping meals so he could squeeze out an extra $10 for Kerry. Another cancelled her daughter's violin lesson to send $50 to the DNC. If the Democratic Party and its candidates ask for this kind of sacrifice from activists, they need to spend the money wisely and account for it. The process needs to be transparent and easy for people to track the money and ensure that it has been properly spent.

And for the most part, candidates and their local campaign staffs uphold their end of the bargain and use the money as smartly as possible. The problem is that millions of small donors are footing the bill for the consultant feast that feeds people like Bob Shrum and his cohorts. To them, these new activist donors are little more than a shiny new ATM to fund the same old campaign.

Even some of the large donors are beginning to recognize this problem of accountability and of overpriced consultants. The Rappaports have been incubating activist groups that merge technology with politics rather than giving money directly to the party committees. "A lot of donors watched the whole debacle with the consultants in the Kerry campaign and saw how all that money got wasted," said Deborah Rappaport. "It was public enough, at least among the donor community, that I think we're going to expect different behavior."

Andy Rappaport sees it as a problem of "an entrenched leadership structure" within the Democratic Party. "We haven't created a parallel leadership structure," he said. "For better or worse, there are still people in positions of leadership and visibility that are still either driven by or represent or are on the side of the consultants. Even though people are becoming a little bit more frustrated or a lot more frustrated, we haven't yet constructed anything else in which they can believe—that's our most important and medium-term challenge. It is to make this not just an intellectual discussion but really to have a parallel leadership structure."

Contrary to the title of Amy Sullivan's article, the consultants didn't get fired. When we sat down with her over drinks in D.C. in October 2005, we asked whether she had heard any updates, particularly about Joe Hansen, one of the main characters in her story. She told us that Hansen is still a partner in the direct-mail firm of Ambrosino, Muir, and Hansen, and still working with the DSCC. He also led a fall training session the DSCC runs for campaign managers. "Even though the DSCC is officially under new management, now run by Chuck Schumer," Sullivan told us, "I've been told that Hansen is close with the staff, particularly the new executive director [J.B. Poersch]."

The consultants have no incentive to change on their own. Regardless of their win-loss record, they've locked campaigns into a certain way of doing business. After Sullivan wrote "Fire the Consultants," the backlash was predictable. "The response was split unevenly," she told us. "On one side were the handful of consultants I named in the piece who reacted angrily, and with good reason, since their jobs depend on being able to line up clients. And on the other side was the rest of Democratic Washington, as well as pockets of frustrated Democrats around the country, who cheered wildly, passed the article around Capitol Hill, and called me to report their favorite evil consultant stories." Of course, some of that enthusiastic response is self-serving. Sullivan "heard some younger, Washington-based former operatives who want Shrum and Mellman swept out of the way so they can set up shop, but would be just as bad, in my opinion. Everyone wants to be a strategist. But what the party needs are consultants who can poll and write direct mail and create memorable ads—there are plenty of those guys outside Washington who have been unfairly shut out of business."

LAYING THE GROUNDWORK

"If you live in Peoria, Illinois, and you're a conservative business guy, you pick up the *Wall Street Journal* and you read the editorial page and you get your stem cell or your Social Security or your 'tort reform' message. If you are a pickup-truck-driving, beer-drinking, 27-year-old, you flip on Rush Limbaugh on the radio. If you're a soccer mom, you watch Bill O'Reilly on Fox. An evangelical listens to Pat Robertson. So every single one of George Bush's voters in Peoria, every segment on any given day can watch, read, or listen to their daily message."

—Rob Stein, cofounder, Democracy Alliance

When the athletes of professional sports teams are playing their best at sporting events, few spectators know or care about the level of preparation it took to get to that level—the network of "farm teams," the coaching, the training, the strategizing, and the selection and care of their equipment.

Politics is no different. Few people, for instance, see the massive machinery that the Right has built, or how it produces the cadre of ideologically steeped, tactically sound candidates and operatives, or what it took to create a noise machine that permeates to the far corners of the country, including Peoria. At least $300 million is spent annually on the coaching, the training, and the selection of message and the development of tactics. And that estimate includes just their expansive network of supposedly "nonpartisan" 501(c)(3) nonprofit organizations, and doesn't include its partisan organizations like Political Action Committees, 527s (political organizations that can raise unregulated "soft" dollars), and issue advocacy groups like the National Rifle Association. On top of this, conservatives also have an equally expansive media machine to cheerlead and promote their efforts.

So when it's show time, be it an election or floor debate in a legislative chamber, Republicans can bring their "A" game—trained, well armed, self-confident, and effective.

Now let's torture the heck out of this sports analogy and look at the Democrats. Let's call them the "Bad News Bears." Coaches and training? There is no coordinated leadership pipeline to train our young stars. Instead, they take advice shouted by their own fans in the stands (the constituency groups). Ideas, tactics and message? There are almost no partisan think tanks to incubate, develop, and provide those crucial elements.

So Democrats stumble out onto the playing field wholly unprepared against their Republican opponents. And they get routed.

THE CONSPIRACY GAP

Never has one of those dreaded PowerPoint presentations brought more notoriety to a man than Rob Stein's did, mainly because it was the first time anyone had quantified and mapped the Vast Right-Wing Conspiracy (VRWC) and graphically shown the enormity of the challenge before the progressive movement. Stein was a former chief of staff under Commerce Secretary Ron Brown in the Clinton administration and later a venture capitalist. His eye-opening forty-slide presentation, titled "The Conservative Message Machine's Money Matrix," was culled from various reports put out by People for the American Way and similar groups as well as from Stein's own sleuthing. And over the past few years, he has shown it to most of the progressive leadership. Matt Bai, writing in the July 25, 2004, issue of the *New York Times Magazine*, described it well:

> The presentation . . . essentially makes the case that a handful
> of families—Scaife, Bradley, Olin, Coors and others—laid the

foundation for a $300 million network of policy centers, advo-
cacy groups and media outlets that now wield great influence
over the national agenda. The network, as Stein diagrams it,
includes scores of powerful organizations—most of them with
bland names like the State Policy Network and the
Leadership Institute—that he says train young leaders and
lawmakers and promote policy ideas on the national and local
level. These groups are, in turn, linked to a massive message
apparatus, into which Stein lumps everything from Fox News
and the *Wall Street Journal* op-ed page to Pat Robertson's *700
Club*. And all of this, he contends, is underwritten by some
200 "anchor donors."

When we talked with Stein at his Arlington, Virginia, office, he
elaborated on that point. "Conservatives have invested in people
who have clarity about ideas, helped create networks with one
another, and have literally populated a movement of people who
think reasonably coherently about a whole wide range of issues and a
set of values," Stein said.

Movement conservatives, including big donors, had been organizing since 1964, when Republican presidential candidate Barry
Goldwater lost by a landslide to Lyndon B. Johnson. For many, it had
been *the* defining moment of their political lives. Goldwater personi-
fied conservative resentment at the Republican establishment's
obsession with being "Democrat-lite," and he rode that frustration
and anger to the 1964 Republican nomination. Two years later,
Goldwater clones started getting elected to office all over the
country, at all levels of government, pushing their conservative ideas.
The spark was lit, and a quiet revolution was underway.

While the true believers organized at campuses, PTA groups, school
boards, state legislatures, and Congress, the big-money conservatives
started dumping hundreds of millions to create their infrastructure.

Think tanks sprung up like weeds. By the time the Scaife-funded Heritage Foundation launched in 1973, it was their eighth think tank focused on economic and foreign policy ideas. Through the 1970s, more such groups were set up, including the American Legislative Exchange Council in 1973 and the libertarian-leaning CATO institute in 1977. By the time Ronald Reagan came on the national scene to run for president against Jimmy Carter in 1980, the conservative movement had about fifteen think tanks pumping out ideas and refining the message. When Reagan won, Heritage gave him a 1,077-page document titled *Mandate for Leadership: Policy Management in a Conservative Administration*, which Reagan promptly handed out to every cabinet member at their first meeting. The antigovernment and pro-privatization document was so detailed that it didn't just promote offshore oil drilling, but specified particular lots that should be exploited. It provided a step-by-step guide on how to transform conservative principles into government policy. It may have been mind-numbingly boring to read, but the paperback version was not only a bestseller inside Washington, D.C., but tangible evidence of the Right's new sophistication—one that had a detailed core set of ideas and policies. Amazingly, Heritage boasts that "nearly two-thirds of the 2,000 recommendations contained in Mandate were adopted by the Reagan administration."

While Reagan ran as an antigovernment Republican in 1980, the conservative machine worked hard through the 1980s and 1990s to create a new agenda for the country, ready for the day that it took over Congress. It was prepared to make the transition from an opposition party providing a bulwark against liberal ruling orthodoxy, to a governing party. "When Reagan and Bush won in the 1980s, they did not have an affirmative agenda for America," notes Stein. "Their agenda was to lower taxes and dismantle the liberal establishment, the structure of government. Get rid of the Office of Economic Opportunity, all these poverty programs, all these Legal Services—

get rid of that shit. It was a deconstruction of liberal institutional capacity. There wasn't an affirmative agenda, a conservative right-wing agenda for America until the Contract with America."

Newt Gingrich's 1994 Contract with America was predicated, not on the dismantling of government, but on creating a government that promoted and instituted conservative principles. "He aggregated all of the work that the infrastructure had been working on—Gingrich didn't come up with a single one of those ideas," Stein said. "Those planks are all work products of the Heritage think tank. That was what they were doing in the 1980s and early 1990s, they were working on these ideas." And not just in D.C., but all around the country, at the state and local levels. So by the time Gingrich pulled it all together in the ten planks of the Contract with America it had been tried and tested through their system. And when Gingrich rode the Contract to a sweeping victory in the House, it was the maturation of the GOP from opposition to governing power. For the first time in six decades, Democrats were shut out of Congress.

Gingrich, and later, George W. Bush and his frighteningly effective brain trust, drew heavily from Marvin Olasky, a product of the Bradley Foundation and author of the 1992 tome *Tragedy of American Compassion*. The antigovernment thesis of Olasky argued that only the faith community, private individuals, and charity organizations could tackle poverty. He dubbed his thesis "compassionate conservatism."

Eight years later, "Bush used that term 'compassionate conservatism,' got elected, and then that affirmative agenda that they had worked on for fifteen years is now everything you see," Stein said. "It's Social Security reform, 'tort reform,' preemption as a military policy, No Child Left Behind, 'Clear Skies,' school vouchers, it's the entire agenda." And if you want any proof that those investments in think tanks and research foundations by the big money conservative donors paid off, simply check out the Heritage Foundation website, where you will find this blurb from Karl Rove: "Heritage is the intellectual centerpiece in Washington for conservative ideas. . . . We stole from every publication we could; we stole several key staff persons; we want to steal more of your ideas."

There is nothing shady about this VRWC, there is nothing illegal about the network of conservative organizations promoting and coordinating their efforts. In fact, what conservatives have built over the past thirty years is nothing short of brilliant. We can admire it the way we would admire the precision, engineering, and craftsmanship of a stealth fighter. That no one even compiled the data on the VRWC, and got the information to the right people until Stein did it in 2003 is an indictment of its own. That the Democratic establishment didn't react to the rise of the VRWC was virtually criminal.

So we lack a vast left-wing conspiracy. Not that it has prevented the wingnuts from fabricating one. One of the most hilarious political books of 2005 was conservative writer Byron York's *The Vast Left Wing Conspiracy*, with the ominous subtitle, *The Untold Story of How Democratic Operatives, Eccentric Billionaires, Liberal Activists, and Assorted Celebrities Tried to Bring Down a President*. By, um, trying to defeat him in a democratic election. The book jacket background helpfully lists the cogs of this VLWC, and it's a pathetic exercise in padding. For example, it lists the Center for American Progress, John Podesta (who runs CAP), David Sirota (who worked at CAP), and the Progress Report (an e-mail newsletter from CAP) all as separate components of this so-called conspiracy. In similar fashion, the author lists MoveOn, Wes Boyd (cofounder of MoveOn), Joan Blades (the other cofounder of MoveOn), and Eli Pariser (head of MoveOn PAC). Poor York couldn't find enough players in our so-called VLWC to fill his book's cover without turning it into an employee directory for the measly few organizations we've got on the ground.

Clearly, we need a real VLWC, one that would allow hacks like York to write a book with some substance in it.

Stein's presentation also generated one of the big paradoxes of the

2004 presidential election. The prospects of a disastrous second term
for Bush (now proven true) generated hundreds of millions of dollars
for John Kerry and Democrats up and down the ballot. Yet many who
saw Stein's presentation knew that regardless of the November results
the progressive movement had a huge, expensive, and difficult task
ahead. A Kerry victory wouldn't erase the massive infrastructure
advantage the Right enjoyed—or the need for the Left to build one
of its own. It would be easier for progressives to begin to build that
infrastructure if Kerry lost. As Anne Bartley, a philanthropist and
board member of the big-dollar-donor group Democracy Alliance,
which was formed after the 2004 elections, told the *Boston Globe* in
June 2005, "Frankly, if Kerry had won, there might not even have
been a Democracy Alliance."

The Alliance, which Stein helped create with Simon Rosenberg
and others, will act as a financial clearinghouse; it will solicit multiyear commitments from major donors and allocate the money to
create and fund a progressive infrastructure of think tanks, media entities, and advocacy groups. By late 2005, the Alliance had tens of millions of dollars in commitments for the next few years. When a history
of this movement is written in a generation or two, the big irony will
be that while Republicans celebrated their 2004 victories, that election actually marked the start of the end of Republican dominance.

THE IDEA FACTORIES

As Stein showed, the conservative movement has built an impressive
array of organizations designed to create the ideas and policies that
shape their ideology and build their message, and ultimately, their
brand. These idea factories include think tanks, state-based policy
organizations, and campus-based institutes and centers: the Heritage
Foundation, the Hoover Institution, the American Enterprise

Institute, the American Legislative Exchange Council (ALEC), the Mercatus Center at George Mason University, and so on. Collectively, these and other institutions spend over $300 million annually developing and marketing the conservative message. Their reach is vast.

To see just how that infrastructure works in practical terms, let's take the example of Michael Krauss, an obscure professor of law at George Mason University. The Commonweal Institute (one of the good guys) tracked his efforts on behalf of "tort reform" interests, and the results are impressive.[51]

Krauss is the author of "Tort Reform, CATO Institute's Handbook for 107th Congress, 2001." Both CATO and George Mason University receive funding from the big conservative families—Scaife, Bradley, Koch, Olin, and Coors. Krauss is also a Salvatori Fellow at the Heritage Foundation, a member of the advisory board of Freedom House, and serves on the board of governors of the National Association of Scholars. All those organizations are funded by some combination of the families listed above. He was previously employed by the Competitive Enterprise Institute, has made various presentations to the conservative lawyer group the Federalist Society, has had his work published and cited in academic journals and publications as well as mainstream right-wing outlets like the *Washington Times* and FoxNews.com.

Even though he's a small cog, at any given moment Krauss' work is being supported by multiple organizations, his ideas are churned through the network of think tanks via their academic publications, and the Right's media outlets help validate and pump out his message to a broader public. Krauss functions within a large matrix that is self-reinforcing and able to identify the best work generated within its confines for transmission nationwide, especially through the halls of power in D.C. and in state capitals. It's a network that exists largely outside of D.C., allowing the conservative movement to use the

states as a laboratory for its ideas. School vouchers, for example, orig-
inated in a Wisconsin think tank, spread to a few states (courtesy of
ALEC), got kicked around their idea factories, received the treat-
ment from language manipulators ("framers," in popular parlance)
like Frank Luntz, hit a few focus groups and polls, and then debuted
on Capitol Hill as a Republican legislative priority.

Yet, while this machine is brutally effective in developing ideas and
turning them into governmental action, it has been a disaster in
turning out *successful* ideas. Consider PNAC, for example.

The Project for a New American Century bills itself as "a nonprofit educational organization dedicated to a few fundamental
propositions: that American leadership is good both for America and
for the world; and that such leadership requires military strength,
diplomatic energy and commitment to moral principle." Established
in 1997, PNAC is also the place, under the tutelage of neocon heavyweights William Kristol and Robert Kagan, where Bush's disastrous
war in Iraq was hatched. In fact, Iraq was an obsession of the PNAC
crew, which included Donald Rumsfeld, Paul Wolfowitz, John
Bolton, and Richard Perle, all of them high-profile members of the
Bush administration. Dick Cheney was a founder. In all, sixteen
members of PNAC were whisked into the Bush administration,
bringing with them their collective body of "research" and conclu-
sions demanding a more aggressive use of military force abroad and
the outright rejection of the United Nations as a mechanism of U.S.
foreign policy. Taking out Saddam Hussein and taking over Iraq was
a top priority. And the 9/11 attacks gave the PNAC gang their excuse
to launch the Iraq War.

Reality has been difficult for the PNAC crew, as we noted in "The
Neocons" section of the first chapter, with the Iraq War turning into
a high-cost, high-body-count disaster with no end in sight. Like so
many ideas crafted in the conservative think tanks (e.g., "tax cuts will
shrink the deficit"), the real world has made a mockery of them.

But no matter how ridiculous or dangerous, the fact remains that conservatives have the institutions to generate ideas. And we don't. "What's your plan?" shout conservatives when we criticize their efforts, and we shrug our shoulders and reply, "Well, not what *you're* doing, that's for sure." Even Kerry's main message in 2004, if he had one, was "I am not George Bush!" For the Americans in the middle, who have no strong partisan allegiances, we have failed to articulate a real plan or vision. And when we have, it has consisted of little more than going back to the way things were done back when we were in power. So, it's either nothing or *That '70s Show*.

The world has changed in the last thirty years, and we need to bring our thinking into the twenty-first century. We must look forward, even while protecting our best accomplishments of the past. We need to bolster the ranks of our think tanks and policy organizations, which are already growing with the likes of the Center for American Progress, Rockridge Institute, Commonweal Institute, Progressive Legislative Action Network, and the New Politics Institute. Beyond the brick-and-mortar organizations, the growing netroots community, including organizations like MoveOn, can aggregate millions of progressives, helping generate, test, and refine ideas better than any focus group.

It's difficult to overstate the need for the Democratic Party to develop its own ideas, not just argue against the Republican ones.

"Democrats think they have all the ideas and they think that the big message machine on the other side is just a 'message machine,' not an idea factory, as they're constantly talking about the message machine as opposed to the idea factory," said George Lakoff, a linguist from Berkeley and author of *Don't Think of an Elephant!* when we met him in July 2005. "But it's the ideas that were crucial to the Republicans; that's why they say they're the party of ideas. And they're right because they've figured out what values they have in common and they started filling in ideas, not just policies. See, the

Democrats don't know the difference between policies and ideas or
policies and values."

Once we have those ideas, we can craft them into our message,
frame them, and, ultimately, build our brand. But without ideas we
have nothing.

THE NOISE MACHINE

On January 7, 2005, *USA Today* reported that conservative columnist
Armstrong Williams had been paid $240,000 by the U.S.
Department of Education to promote the Bush administration's "No
Child Left Behind" law. Working through the PR firm of Ketchum
Inc., the federal agency paid Williams to "promote the law on his
nationally syndicated television show and to urge other black journalists to do the same," the newspaper reported. "The campaign, part
of an effort to promote No Child Left Behind (NCLB), required com-
mentator Armstrong Williams 'to regularly comment on NCLB
during the course of his broadcasts,' and to interview Education
Secretary Rod Paige for TV and radio spots that aired during the
show in 2004."

The agreement was not only a violation of journalistic ethics but,
as the General Accounting Office pointed out, it was a violation of
the law that bans government "propaganda" and lobbying efforts on
behalf of legislation. Williams lost his syndicated column with
Tribune Media Services, earned the scorn of his peers, and was suddenly a bona fide distraction to the Bush administration. Bush
spokesperson Scott McClellan faced repeated questions over several
days about the propaganda arrangement, and by the end of January,
investigative reporters dug up additional conservative media persons
on the public dole—syndicated columnist Maggie Gallagher was
busted for taking money from the Department of Health and Human

Services to promote Bush's "Healthy Marriage" initiative, while syndicated columnist Michael McManus was paid to promote a federal marital counseling program.

The conservative media machine had to divert attention, and do so quickly. And it found the perfect targets for its new smear campaign—the two of us.

The goal was to claim moral equivalence—that the administration's propaganda efforts were no big deal because Democrats do it too. Fortunately for the right-wing machine, an obscure blog post for an obscure conference by Zephyr Teachout, a former campaign staffer for Howard Dean's presidential bid, gave them the ammunition they needed. In her now-defunct blog, Teachout wrote that the campaign "paid Markos and Jerome Armstrong as consultants, largely in order to ensure that they said positive things about Dean." She also added this: "To be very clear, they never committed to supporting Dean for the payment—but it was very clearly, internally, our goal."

However, as Dean campaign manager Joe Trippi noted in response, if that was their goal, it was a pretty darn stupid one. Jerome quit blogging and the Dean campaign lost perhaps their greatest champion in the netroots. And Markos put up a disclaimer top and center on his blog. Furthermore, the payments were for technical services, and were not from taxpayer money. But the storyline was good enough for a smear of equivalency.

It didn't matter that Teachout's claims were refuted by Trippi, by Dean's internet communications director Mathew Gross, and by Dean spokesperson Laura Gross (no relation to Mathew). The opening salvo was a hit piece from the *Wall Street Journal*, published on January 14, seven days after the original Williams story broke. Writers Bill Bulkeley and James Bandler cobbled together an article so sloppy that media watchdogs almost instantly debunked it. The *Columbia Journalism Review* handed out its first ever "Lipstick on a Pig Award" to the *WSJ* for that story's gross sensationalism.[52]

But the machine was in motion with lightning speed and it wouldn't stop. Conservative gossipmonger Matt Drudge, the source of first resort for all right-wing smear bombs, trumpeted the so-called scandal on his website. Conservative blogger Glenn Reynolds of InstaPundit, then the most-trafficked right-wing blog, fueled its transmission throughout the right side of blog world. The conservative rag *The Weekly Standard* ran with it. By the end of the day on January 14, radio blowhard Hugh Hewitt had latched on to it, and was talking it up with Bill O'Reilly on Fox News:

> **HUGH HEWITT, "BLOG" AUTHOR:** Bloggers on the take are very bad for the business of blogging. Bloggers are real journalists and people like Powerline and like InstaPundit, like myself, we don't like it when Daily Kos shows up on the take of the Howard Dean campaign. Now Daily Kos says—this is one of the bloggers from the left—he disclosed it, but not to the satisfaction of anyone who was watching. I didn't know.
> **O'REILLY:** Oh, this is bunk. This is bull. Nobody knew about this.
> **HEWITT:** That's right.

They "didn't know." And they figured "nobody knew." This despite there being at least fifteen news stories during Dean's campaign noting Markos' consulting agreement, including such headlines as "Dean Consultant in Berkeley Builds 'Blog' Into Influential Tool" a year previously in the January 15, 2004, edition of the *San Francisco Chronicle*.

Within twenty-four hours of the *Wall Street Journal* story, the right-wing noise machine had propelled it into the corporate media nationwide. Stories discussing the Armstrong Williams scandal started including references to "revelations" that "Dean bloggers" had their own "pay for play" scheme. Fox News Channel ran it as "breaking news." CNN anchor Kelly Wallace, interviewing Tim

Roemer that same day about the DNC chairman's race—Roemer was Dean's rival in seeking that post—asked for comment, describing it as a story where we were paid to "say positive things" about Dean. And the next morning, *Washington Post* media critic Howard Kurtz, was there to wrap it all up.

What was a real scandal of Bush and the Republicans using taxpayer money for propaganda was turned within one day into a story about how "everyone does it."

A few months later, the story continued to linger, with an ironic twist at Columbia University, where journalism professor Steve Ross included the example of "bloggers getting paid by the Dean campaign" in an ethics survey sent out to journalists. When we confronted Ross with the error, his e-mail response to us was extremely telling: "I had a bunch of examples that seemed antibusiness and anti-Republican so I wanted something different."

There's no doubt, as our personal experience demonstrated vividly, that the Right dominates the media. Arbitron ratings put Rush Limbaugh's radio audience at twenty million listeners a week. Conservatives dominate cable news, with an overtly partisan network in Fox News Channel, and a slate of on-air right-wing personalities on MSNBC and CNBC that far outnumber their centrist and liberal counterparts. The Sunday morning talk shows are stacked by conservative voices, as regularly reported by the media watchdog group Media Matters for America.

Cries of "liberal media" ring increasingly hollow, to the point that even the odious Ann Coulter admitted on Sean Hannity's show that "we have the media now." The Right has overtly partisan outfits like the *Washington Times*, the *Wall Street Journal's* editorial board, Pat Robertson's *700 Club*, Eagle Publishing, and a network of hyperpartisan web publications like *NewsMax* and the *Free Republic*. The conservative propaganda machine even includes allowing their ilk into hollowed journalistic ground, such as the White House briefing room. While supposedly limited to reporters from major news organizations, the Bush White House allowed gay sex escort Jim Guckert—masquerading as a "reporter" for a conservative news organization hilariously called "Talon News"—to cover news conferences without the requisite FBI background checks. In fact, his press credentials listed a fake name—Jeff Gannon. No official explanation has been given for how Guckert managed to acquire credentials.

At the beginning of this decade, the liberal media landscape was bleak. Even so-called liberal editorial boards at the *Washington Post* and the *New York Times* were infected with war fever, eagerly cheering Bush's unwarranted invasion of Iraq and looking the other way when it came to the spectacular mismanagement of the budget and the economy. In fact, one of the few bright spots was the liberal blogosphere, then a speck of dust in a hostile media landscape.

But the blogs grew at astronomical rates. Daily Kos, the largest political blog in the world, has been growing steadily at a clip of 5 to 10 percent every *week*, and by fall 2005 was getting over a million visits every day—more than the top fifty conservative blogs *combined*. The rest of the progressive blogosphere has been no slouch either, far outpacing the growth of its conservative foes.[53]

We have also started growing liberal radio after the upstart Air America and Democracy Radio networks made a mockery of radio behemoth Clear Channel's assertions that talk radio would never work. Now, the conservative, publicly traded company is adding liberal talk radio across its nationwide network of stations as a growth niche while conservative talk radio stagnates. Liberal talk show host Ed Schultz of North Dakota has grown to over one hundred markets in just a year. And while television is still no-man's land for liberals, at least one venture fund has sprung up to bring overtly liberal programming to cable and even broadcast television.

NO INVESTMENT, NO RETURN

The Leadership Institute, based in Arlington, Virginia, and founded in 1979, proudly proclaims on its website that its mission is to "identify, recruit, train, and place conservatives in politics, government, and media." It is an $8-million-a-year operation (funded by the Coors family and others[54]), but this group is under constant threat of self-parody. According to them, liberals want to "tax all income at 100%," believe that "traditional morality is always bad," want to "break all family ties," "make God illegal," and "save the environment . . . Kill off all the people."

Their president, Morton Blackwell, was the man behind those "purple heart Band-Aids" that so-called patriotic attendees to the Republican National Convention in 2004 wore to mock John Kerry's heroic Vietnam War service. With an enrollment of over 40,000 since the group's inception in 1979, its alumni listing is a veritable who's who of the conservative movement, including Grover Norquist, president of Americans for Tax Reform; Karl Rove; former Christian Coalition wunderkind Ralph Reed; 233 legislators and members of Congress; right-wing bloggers; and even two former Miss America titleholders.

Their curriculum spans everything from classes on "How to stop liberals in their tracks," to classes on conservative media, candidate development, public speaking, and how to score jobs on Capitol Hill. Their youth training programs include workshops on winning campus elections and taking over campus newspapers. And post-training, the Leadership Institute helps its alumni find jobs.

Peter Murray, who is trying to replicate the Leadership Institute's efforts on the Left with his new Center for Progressive Leadership, which was one of the first organizations to receive funding from the Democracy Alliance, noted to Salon.com in a story dated May 24, 2005: "We spent $2 billion trying to win this last election. [The

Leadership Institute] already spent 25 years, and nearly $100 million, building the talent pool that won the election. And which will consistently win them elections for the next several decades."

Conservatives have dropped a mint on developing the leaders of the future at places like the Leadership Institute. Young People for the American Way, an offshoot of the People for the American Way Foundation, has tracked eleven conservative leadership, training, and mentoring organizations that operate in high schools, colleges, and law schools with a combined budget of nearly $36 million in 2003 and $45 million in 2004.

The Left does have a fair number of organizations—including Camp Wellstone, Democratic Gain, Progressive Majority, Emily's List, and so on—that train campaign workers. Most issue groups have a training arm as well, such as GreenCorps, Gloria Steinem Leadership Institute, Choice USA, and so on, but they are a different beast than what the Right has built. Iara Peng, one of the progressive movement's top young stars and head of Young People for the American Way, looks at these progressive groups and finds them significantly different from the right's leadership organizations. "Are they collaborative? No. Are they long-term? No. Do they work with an individual over the course of their careers? No," said Peng. "Can just anybody find out about these institutes and just take a course? Get trained? Not really. At least not without lots of money—usually conferences/trainings cost so much you only get older white people attending."

The other side works differently. "The Right molds and shapes leaders, especially in media, like Dinesh D'Souza, Tucker Carlson, Ann Coulter, Ralph Reed, and others. Their leadership programs are a leadership pipeline," says Peng. Karl Rove was president of the College Republicans in 1975, Grover Norquist held the post in 1981, and Ralph Reed held the subsequent two-year term through 1983. The Right was able to run them through its leadership machine for their "education," and they eventually emerged as influential figures in the conservative movement. By contrast, College Democrats fall off the face of the earth after graduation since there is no progressive machine to train and mentor them. "Young People For and others like the Center for Progressive Leadership are laying the groundwork to build this 'machine' but we are in the design and incubation stages," said Peng. "We are here for the long term, but we are, for the most part, just getting started." Peng's organization had an inaugural class of 126 fellows from 40 colleges and universities and a budget of just under $1 million. The 2006 class was scheduled to grow to 165 fellows who are taught how to engage in advocacy politics and given resources to carry it out.

Murray's Center for Progressive Leadership, established in 2004, has a budget barely topping $1 million. It has set up shop in Arizona, Michigan, and Pennsylvania, and hopes to continue expanding in more states. In October 2005, the Democracy Alliance selected CPL as one of its charter beneficiaries, which could drive its budget closer to $3 million. Murray hopes to revolutionize the whole field. "If I was a conservative donor of the Leadership Institute I would be pissed as hell. Despite all their successes, they haven't spent the money well. They haven't learned from the corporate sector," Murray told us. A central tenet of his training philosophy is the concept of "executive coaching"—common in the corporate and nonprofit world (a $1 billion industry, used by over half of all businesses[55]) but nonexistent in the political world, including the conservative side.

That's the progressive hope. But the current gap is readily apparent, as it was to reporter Jason DeParle, who began his story in the June 14, 2005, *New York Times* about the Heritage Foundation's internship program with this:

> They are young and bright and ardently right. They tack
> Ronald Reagan calendars on their cubicle walls and devote

brown bag lunches to the free market theories of Friedrich von Hayek. They come from 51 colleges and 28 states, calling for low taxes, strong defense and dorm rooms with a view. And let's get one thing straight: they're not here to run the copying machine.

The summer interns of the Heritage Foundation have arrived, forming an elite corps inside the capital's premier conservative research group. The 64 interns are each paid a 10-week stipend of $2,500, and about half are housed in a subsidized dorm at the group's headquarters, complete with a fitness room.

. . . It is an alternative with few rivals. The Brookings Institution, a centrist group more than 50 years older than Heritage, has no paid interns. Neither does the Progressive Policy Institute, which promotes a centrist version of liberalism. The Center on Budget and Policy Priorities, a premier antipoverty group, has 10 paid interns. People for the American Way, a bulwark of Beltway liberalism, has 40 [typically unpaid]—but no dorm.

Providing housing doesn't just allow young conservatives from all walks of life to serve as interns in D.C. (liberals need to be "trust fund babies" to afford unpaid internships at progressive organizations in pricey D.C.), but it allows them to start networking early in their career. Progressives at D.C.-based organizations are viewed more as low-cost or no-cost employees, and when their internships end, they go back to where they came from. They're not seen as an investment for the future. They are not formally mentored. And they're not placed in real jobs at the end of the internships.

Training and mentoring our young stars takes added importance on the electoral front. Fifty percent of all high-level office holders were elected to their first office before the age of thirty-five. And once elected, they hold all manner of advantages over their unelected foes—the benefits of incumbency, experience campaigning, and a growing fundraising network. Republicans are taking care of their young stars, funneling them into places where they can have the most impact, be it academia, the punditry, media, or elected office, while we starve our young.

Two quick examples can shed some light on this disparity.

The first is Naomi Schaefer Riley, not quite a household name. She is deputy Taste-Page editor at the *Wall Street Journal*, working in the paper's leisure section. Her bio when she was still working at the Ethics and Public Policy Center, is Exhibit A in how the Right takes care of its young stars.

> Ms. Riley is a contributing writer at *The American Enterprise* and a frequent contributor to the *Wall Street Journal*, the *Boston Globe*, and *National Review*. Her articles have also appeared in the *Weekly Standard*, *The New Republic*, *Commentary*, *Crisis*, the *Public Interest*, and *First Things*. Since graduating from Harvard magna cum laude in 1998, she has worked as assistant editor of *Commentary*, as well as an editorial intern at the *Wall Street Journal* editorial page and *National Review*. She has been the recipient of the Phillips Foundation Journalism Fellowship, the Intercollegiate Studies Institute Journalism Fellowship, the Claremont Institute Publius Fellowship, and the Charles G. Koch Fellowship.[56]

Her book, *God on the Quad: How Religious Colleges Are Changing America*, received grants from four conservative institutions—the Templeton Foundation, the Randolph Foundation, the Phillips Foundation, and the John M. Olin Foundation. This young writer has received financial support from no less than eight conservative foundations and has been published in no less than seven conservative publications. And now she has a plum assignment at the *Wall Street Journal*, doing the kind of fluff work that will allow her to keep writing books and publishing in lower-paying conservative publications. There's nothing wrong with that, and in fact it's quite admirable. It's how movements grow—by taking care of their young stars and ensuring a steady supply of new leaders for the future.

Now compare Riley to Sharon Lettman, a thirty-six-year-old African American activist.

"When I was in college, every door was open. I was regarded as an all-star who chose to attend a black college," Lettman told us in an e-mail exchange. "I had it all—travel, awards, speeches, and national recognition. Many thought I would be an elected official. [From] 18–23, I could do no wrong. But after 23, it was as if every door shut. There were no upwardly mobile career opportunities in the progressive movement. No support structures to launch me in the social justice arena. So I made my own way and became a successful entrepreneur." That is, until People for the American Way snatched her up following the 2000 election debacle in Florida.

Ralph Neas, president of PAW, considers Lettman a huge score for his organization, but laments the circuitous route she had to take to put her considerable talents to work for the progressive movement. "[After she graduated from college], no one tried to get her into academia, in grad school, or law school. No one tried to get her placed in a newspaper, at the *Washington Times* equivalent the way that the Right does at the *Wall Street Journal* and elsewhere. No one takes care of the young progressives. They're supposed to fend for themselves and eventually they'll come back or be part of us. But the Right doesn't do it that way. They are going to Morton Blackwell's Leadership Institute and they're being placed and they're being funded. It's night and day. It's just night and day."

REAL INCOME VS. PSYCHIC INCOME

Without a doubt, there is very little mentorship in progressive organizations, because the money and the attitude are both lacking. They treat employees as though they should be happy to work in something "meaningful," even if it means living in poverty. There is an institutional hostility toward paying professionals—activists, writers, researchers, organizers, PR staffers, fundraisers, and so on—market rates for their work.

"Even the sweetest, most progressive family foundations do not want to pay for salaries," said Amy Kiser, development director for the nonprofit Ecology Center in Berkeley, California. "There is a preference for all-volunteer projects, and I'm guessing that speaks to some sort of purity."

The Right has no such attitudes. Many of the leaders come from the business world and understand the power of money to motivate and focus people. Rob Stein estimates that of the top eighty organizations he has studied in the VRWC, there are about 2,000 conservative leaders earning between $75,000 and $200,000. The Leadership Institute's Blackwell made $187,433 in salary in 2004, his top five lieutenants clocked in between $88,066 and $130,744. At Focus on the Family, the top five compensated employees earned between $78,411 and $106,856 in 2004. The pay is good, ensuring they keep their brightest and best, and creates a draw for talent from outside the conservative movement. No one ever failed to pay their rent or gave up eating out because they worked at a conservative organization.

On our side, we face a steady stream of defections to the private sector where the pay is far better. As Napoleon said, an army travels on its stomach, a lesson progressive leaders have yet to learn. We train them young, teach them the ropes, and as they reach the age where they could take a more active leadership role in the movement, they decide they can't live with six roommates, default on their student loans, and eat Ramen noodles for dinner every night. They decide they want things like a car in good working order, they want to own a home, and they want to feel that their efforts are properly compensated. And the low pay also fails to lure committed people from the private sector. "People want to get out of the private sector and do work for them that feels karmically good to them," said Kiser. "But when they see how much it pays they are shocked. It keeps them out."

One of the big ironies is that progressive funders—who bear much of the fault for encouraging slave wages in progressive organizations—often run their own businesses or invest in for-profit ventures. And they would never treat their own employees in that manner.

"I think that what's happened is that donors have developed two different brains," Andy Rappaport explained to us when we met him in Redwood City, California, in August 2005. "There's our business brain, which holds our kind of rational, no-nonsense 'This is how I earn my living, this is the way the world works' kind of stuff. And then there's our touchy-feely brain that deals with all of the social and political—and I think this is truer for the left than for the right, obviously. Progressive donors hold nonprofits to different standards and they don't naturally think about the application of things that many of us have learned in our for-profit endeavors to nonprofits.

"So, for example, you think that nonprofits are doing good work and so therefore, people do it because they love it, whereas if I were a partner in a law firm and I were trying to hire an associate and said 'Well, this person must be a lawyer because he or she loves it and it's good work and so therefore they'll work for nothing,' I would probably not have a very successful law firm."

Deborah Rappaport doesn't buy the notion of "psychic income"— that good work is its own reward. "Everybody's looking to try to figure out what the lessons are to learn from the past forty years of the Republican Party, which I think in a lot of senses is a fool's errand at this point," she said. "But one of the things that I think we can learn is the professionalization of the organizations and the workers in those organizations. It's not just 'Because you're doing good work, you should get psychic income.' It's 'We value it, we respect it, we have high expectations of you and therefore we're going to compensate you appropriately.'"

As we build our infrastructure and help reform our existing institutions, the issue of activist/employee compensation must be addressed. The Rappaports have been working on that front, even seeking ways to offer such basics as health insurance to professional activists, and other donors have voiced similar commitments to a well-compensated progressive activist corps. Whether that becomes the norm at progressive organizations remains to be seen.

"Don't think of this as a charity, think of this as an organization that has to be effective in conducting its mission. Can this organization be effective if it can't recruit and retain the best possible talent?" Andy Rappaport asks. "Well, if it has to compete with industry for the best possible talent, yeah, maybe somebody will work for 10 percent less, or maybe they'll work for a salary and no stock options, maybe they won't. But they're not going to work for 50 percent less and they're not going to work if there's only three months of funding in the bank."

On top of low pay, there is no support structure for nurturing, mentoring, and absorbing our best talent into progressive organizations. Neas sees it all the time. "What the other side has done so well is invest in young people. They cultivate them early on, I think in high school but certainly in college. And Young Republicans are really a force at colleges while the Federalist Society is an extraordinary force at the law schools," he said. "But, they just don't cultivate them, they don't just train them; they get them jobs, they get them stipends, they get them placed in academia, they get them placed on Capitol Hill, they get them placed in journalism. They're always cultivating, they're always mentoring and they take care of them and they promote them."

Until the Sharon Lettmans on our side are treated as well as the
Naomi Rileys on their side, we will suffer a human deficit. We need
a professional movement that treats its people as well as Microsoft
and Google, that rewards them based on the market value of their
talent and skills, and that generally believes that old saying that "you
get what you pay for."

SEED MONEY

To hear conservatives talk, the Democratic Party is bought and paid
for by George Soros. Despite the fact that he only put in about $27
million of the $1 billion Democrats spent in the 2004 election cycle,
Soros has become the bogeyman for the right wing.[57] Republican
House Speaker Dennis Hastert suggested on the August 29, 2004,
edition of *Fox News Sunday* that Soros was a drug smuggler: "You
know, I don't know where George Soros gets his money. I don't know
where—if it comes overseas or from drug groups or where it comes
from." The very next day, Newt Gingrich went on the *Hannity &
Colmes* show on Fox and charged that Soros "wants to spend $75 mil-
lion defeating [President] George W. Bush because Soros wants to
legalize heroin." Less than three months earlier, radio host Michael
Savage had compared Soros to "Hitler's media man" (Soros is a Jew
that survived the Nazi occupation of his native Hungary). Savage
called Soros a "lousy snake" and a "money changer in the temple of
truth," and called MoveOn.org, a beneficiary of Soros' largesse, "an
organization of rat-bastard communists."[58] That savage attack came a
day after Tony Blankley, the editorial page editor of the *Washington
Times* went on *Hannity & Colmes* and unleashed a torrent of abusive
language on Soros, including calling him "a left-wing crank," "a Jew
who figured out a way to survive the Holocaust," "a robber baron"
and "a pirate capitalist."[59]

The singular obsession with Soros has, in many ways, masked the rise of a new generation of donors to progressive causes, from grassroots and netroots first-time donors, to millionaire and billionaire first-time donors.

According to OpenSecrets.org, the web site of the Center for Responsive Politics, Democrats spent nearly $1.9 billion on federal races in the 2004 election cycle—$326 million by the Kerry campaign and $168 million by the other Democratic presidential primary challengers, $295 million by the DNC, $302 million by candidates for the U.S. House, and $247 million for Senate candidates. Allied progressive groups—527s and PACs—added over $500 million.

Post-election money has been tight, putting a great number of progressive organizations in financial difficulty. America Coming Together, which ran the "get out the vote" operation in about a dozen battleground states and spent nearly $85 million doing so, has already closed its doors.[60] Many chalk it up to the inevitable downsizing of a postelection year. But there are signs of change as several groups have risen to the challenge. One is an unnamed, informal billionaires club, led by George Soros.[61] The D.C.-based Democracy Alliance (formerly led by Rob Stein) is another, as is the Silicon Valley–based New Progressive Coalition run by the Rappaports. In the 2004 election cycle, Andy and Deborah Rappaport pumped $7 million into organizations like People for the American Way and New Democrat Network while incubating startups like the youth-oriented Music for America and PunkVoter.com, as well as CivicSpace, an effort to create a free-to-low-cost suite of internet tools for political campaigns. This year, they are already big donors in the startup New Politics Institute. The New World Foundation is working to set up the New Majority Fund, a $40 million bank designed to reach and fund grassroots organizations.

There is a bit of a cultural divide between the East Coast and West Coast donors. The East Coast groups are playing the New

York financier role—funding established organizations, while the Rappaports' Silicon Valley mind-set shines through in the startups they are helping finance. But the goals are similar and complementary—to create and bolster our own infrastructure separate from the Democratic Party machinery. At an April 2005 meeting bringing many of these donors together, party consultants were kept away, as the Capitol Hill newspaper *The Hill* reported. "[Democracy Alliance] is not beholden to the political calendar, and several sources insisted that four-year electoral exigencies were not motivating the project. Indeed, part of the reasoning in keeping D.C. consultants away from Scottsdale was to shield the high-tech donor base from political operatives, who are always eager for quick dollars to buy media points and fund direct mail."[62]

However, the tens of millions the big donors can raise annually pales in comparison to what small donors can raise on their own.

The MoveOn.org Voter Fund raised $17 million in 2004—$11 million of it from 160,000 donors with an average $69 contribution.[63] Howard Dean's DNC, which has broken party records for fundraising the year following a presidential election, had raised $42.4 million the first three quarters of 2005. The DNC has launched a "Democracy Bonds" campaign to recruit 500,000 people to pledge $20 a month in recurring donations—enough to offset the $10 million the RNC receives monthly. They've signed up 25,000 thus far. And the Rappaport's New Progressive Coalition will aggressively recruit small-dollar donors to supplement the big dollars raised. If done right, it will be the big-dollar donors supplementing the small donors.

There are lessons we can learn from Republicans about how to use our money wisely. First and foremost, we must build organizations and fund operations that go beyond the next election cycle. "They don't just spend $300 million, but they do it over the long term. And most funders give to at least two organizations working in similar fields," explains Peng. "That reduces competition and increases collaboration and effectiveness."

And, as discussed in the second chapter, the focus on single-issue groups at the expense of a broad progressive movement must be transformed. "There might be a lot of money going to environmental organizations and NARAL and Planned Parenthood, but in the current political environment this money is largely wasted," says Dave Johnson, a research fellow at the Commonweal Institute. "If those organizations were working to change the political environment by reaching the general public with a more general pro-progressive education effort, their own interests would be better served. Meanwhile the major funders—foundations, etc.—only fund specific, narrow 'programs' and refuse to provide money for 'advocacy' and for general operating expenses that would allow the organizations to reach out past their base."

Funding the infrastructure cannot happen fast enough. Democrats need the institutions, they need trained activists, and most of all, they need the institutions and the activists to develop ideas, to articulate a vision, to have a real brand.

Right now, the problem is that Democrats are mostly playing defense. We're running around defending Social Security, defending the Arctic National Wildlife Refuge, defending *Roe v. Wade*, and so on. Noble and crucial causes, no doubt, but they're not ideas, they're not visionary, they're not forward thinking, and they're certainly not "progressive" in the literal sense of that word, as in "promoting progress." We're basically defending the status quo that is under constant threat from the reactionary Right.

So in a (very ironic) way, we have become the conservative party, while Republicans are the progressive party, using government to bring about social change. That's a painful admission to make.

Yet we should take heart in the fact that Democrats consistently lose elections only *narrowly*, which means that despite the massive advantages of the right-wing machine and their hundreds of millions of dollars, we are still the party of the people. We just need to prep our troops in the finer arts of political warfare—train them, give them the tools, tactics and message—and allow them to add their own personalized ideas and emphasis on to the party's brand. We need our own media machine to support progressives and help set the national agenda so we're not always responding to right-wing attacks.

In practical terms, Democratic candidates start at a serious disadvantage to their Republican opponents. By the time an election comes along, voters already know what Republicans stand for and what their issues are, so their campaigns can focus on reinforcing the GOP message and building name recognition. Our candidates must work on the name recognition stuff as well, but in the absence of a coherent party message or brand, they must start from scratch and explain their views and what values they hold dear. Not only does that require extra energy, money, and effort, but it also allows Republican opponents to "define" our candidates with the negative aspects of the Democratic brand ("baby killer," "tree hugger," and so on). And since every Democrat is running on a different message, it reinforces the notion that Democrats have no shared core principles.

If electoral campaigns are a 100-meter dash, then Republicans have a 50-meter head start. That's one reason why their worst candidates can get elected, while Democrats need extraordinary ones to win.

Building infrastructure isn't the sexiest topic. To quote the current president of the United States, "it's hard work." It's expensive. It's a daunting task because we're essentially starting from zero. But it must be done. More than anything else, the long-term future of the progressive movement depends on building this infrastructure.

CIVIL WAR

"In the beginning of a change the patriot is a scarce man, and brave, and hated and scorned. When his cause succeeds, the timid join him, for then it costs nothing to be a patriot."

—Mark Twain

To paraphrase Thomas Jefferson, the tree of a political party must be refreshed from time to time with the blood of reformers and insiders. Any entrenched class will grow fat, lazy, and corrupt, unable or unwilling to adapt to change, and will fight for its perks and privileges. It's the natural order of things. The Democratic Party has long since reached that point where it must be "refreshed"—it is virtually impotent, yet self-satisfied, in the face of the havoc that Republicans are wreaking on our country.

A whole new generation of reformers—from the online world of the netroots, to new multi-issue groups, to new labor, to new big-dollar donors—is engaged in a two-front war: battling to knock Republicans off their perch while jostling for control of the Democratic Party.

For their part, the powers that be within the Democratic Party are eyeing the landscape nervously, trying to figure out what to do—bow to the inevitable, get out of the game, or put up a fight. Just since 2003, we've seen several skirmishes between the reform movement and the Democratic political establishment.

But before we get to those skirmishes, let's take a quick look at how this balance of power within the Democratic Party began to shift—and why. For us, the spark is clear—it was the McCain-Feingold campaign finance reform law (CFR). The day after the 2002 midterm elections, the McCain-Feingold law took effect banning the use of "soft money"—donations larger than $2,000 for individuals, or $5,000 by political action committees. Thanks to the efforts of Democratic senator Russ Feingold of Wisconsin and Republican senator John McCain of Arizona, the Democratic Party was about to go broke because it was deprived—literally overnight—of the million-dollar donations that had sustained its efforts for decades.

For party leaders and operatives, having the "soft money" pipeline turned off was terrifying. The 1974 amendments to the Federal Election Campaign Act held an exemption to the hard-dollar limits allowing contributions of unlimited amounts for "party building" efforts. This was the loophole that enabled the party apparatus to raise millions from corporations or individuals, especially for presidential campaigns. The Democratic National Committee (DNC) used more than $17 million to fund "issue ads" in the spring of 1996 to influence the presidential race. Both parties exploited the loophole. According to OpenSecrets.org, donors such as Arnold Hiatt and Miriam Cannon Hayes gave $500,000 to the DNC and RNC, respectively, in the 1996 cycle. Handing over more than $100,000 to the DNC would grant you a seat on its "Executive Council"; the same amount turned over to the RNC would make you a player in their "Team 100." Rather than build the party, these large donations decimated the Democratic Party's donor base. Gradually, from the 1980s through the 1990s and into the 2000s, the Democratic Party increasingly ignored the small donors and relied instead upon big-dollar contributions to fund its campaign operations. It was easier for the Democrats in D.C. to secure a single $1 million check, than it was to garner $20 each from 50,000 people.

The Republican Party was fine—it had built its financial dominance on the strength of a successful direct-mail operation that netted hundreds of millions in small-dollar donations. But Democrats had more to fear. Democrats found themselves in an odd dilemma: they were publicly in favor of campaign finance reform and getting big money out of government, but they also did not want to have a law that hurt them much more than it hurt the Republicans. Seen through the prism of that time, the legislation meant unilateral disarmament against the GOP. Many in the Democratic establishment believed McCain-Feingold was a death knell for the party.

A report in the July 11, 2001, *Washington Post* laid bare the Democratic fears: "'The party is putting a gun to its head and it's about to pull the trigger, and members don't even know that the gun is loaded,' said one Democratic strategist. 'This is going to have a devastating effect on the ability to elect Democrats. . . . There is absolute unanimity on the part of the Democratic consulting community that this bill is a disaster for Democrats.'" (Yup. The same consulting geniuses we talked about in the third chapter.) Some Republicans, rubbing their hands in gleeful anticipation, referred to the bill as the "Democratic Party suicide bill," a moniker that ended up as a headline of an *Atlantic Monthly* article in the July 1, 2003, issue.

Senator Hillary Clinton and Feingold sparred over the legislation, as reported by the *New York Daily News* on July 18, 2002. At a closed-door Senators' luncheon at the Capitol, the possibility of legal challenges by Republicans to Democrats' fundraising efforts was brought up. When Feingold dismissed such speculation, Clinton "exploded," the newspaper said, and shouted, "Russ, live in the real world!" Feingold stood his ground. While Clinton and Feingold reportedly made nice later with apologies all around, a Democratic source told *Roll Call*, "It was riveting—it was wonderful. It was like a genie out of the bottle—somebody actually told Russ Feingold to go fuck himself."[64] (*Roll Call* omitted the expletive.) Feingold told *Roll Call* that at least five other senators also "threw a fit."

Feingold told us that he knew he was stepping on toes inside his own party, but he saw no choice. "The purpose of McCain-Feingold really was only one, and it's that there was blatant corruption going on here" that needed to end, Feingold said, gesturing to the DSCC conference room in Washington, D.C., where we were talking. "When somebody asks for a $500,000 contribution here and then walks across the street and votes on that company's bill, that is, in my view, inherently corrupt. And certainly, as the Supreme Court said, if not corrupt, it gives the appearance of corruption."

This being politics, those $500,000 donations Feingold talked about are still coming in, except now they go to a new breed of political organizations, the 527s—named after the section of the tax code under which they are organized. They operate outside the purview of the Federal Election Commission and can influence the outcome of elections as long as they don't explicitly advocate the election or defeat of any candidate for federal office. But the party and its candidates no longer have access to the big dollars, and if nothing else, the *appearance* of corruption has been reduced.

Still, that accomplishment pales in comparison to the law's real accomplishment—forcing the Democratic Party to reconnect to real people.

Given the new campaign finance rules, the Democratic Party would either go the way of the Whigs—as the party's leadership and its "consulting community" feared—or it would turn to the people it claimed to represent to help fund its operations. And as it turned out, the latter happened as the party reached out to its rank and file for the first time in decades. Suddenly, organizations and entities that could deliver small-dollar donors were relevant and in hot demand, from the MoveOn folks to the bloggers to grassroots Democrats previously taken for granted.

"Bill Clinton was a great fundraiser, but the Democratic Party wasn't going to be the party of money and the party of people," said

Feingold. "We are the party of the people, because if we're not, then we're nobody. Unless our power is based on numbers of people, and committed enthusiasm of people, we'll never win, because we're never going to win the soft-money game."

Feingold faced down his party and forced it to reconnect with its base. And all that animosity from the Democratic establishment toward Feingold seems to have faded. . "Now we're getting along fine, because it's a new era and I think they've finally realized that the future of this party is more with what *you* guys are doing than it is with trying to cozy up to the relatively modest number of extremely, ridiculously wealthy Democrats," he said.

Campaign finance reform was the first skirmish between reformers and the comfortably numb establishment, and once the bill became law, it upended the established order of the political world. But no one saw it coming. Not until an unknown governor from an obscure New England state burst onto the national scene.

THE DEAN MACHINE

Howard Dean was an unlikely revolutionary figure. As governor of Vermont from 1991 to 2003, he was a consensus builder who was fiscally conservative and socially progressive. He planned on running a health-care-focused presidential primary campaign. Nobody gave him much of a chance. The battle was expected to be between staid establishment candidates like Senator Joe Lieberman, Senator John Kerry, and House Minority Leader Dick Gephardt. But a confluence of events—the Democratic rollover on Bush's Iraq misadventures and the rise of the then-tiny but vocal blogging community—conspired to catapult Dean into improbable front-runner status.

It began quietly enough, with Dean's campaign building under-the-radar netroots support for months over the internet, tapping into a frustration over the lack of opposition to Bush by complacent Democrats. On March 15, 2003, when he spoke at California's annual state Democratic Party gathering at the convention center in Sacramento, Dean was still registering below 5 percent nationally in the polls. We were there expecting the usual Republican-lite speeches, but hoping for more. The evening before, we had watched John Kerry give a "keynote address" that was so long and failed on so many levels it was tragically comic—the convention hall lighting was too dim, the speaker system never worked, and Kerry made bad jokes about his prostate. The crowd milled around uninterested while Kerry labored on, his wife Theresa fidgeting by his side. The next afternoon, a prerecorded address from Joe Lieberman provoked hissing from the generally liberal crowd. John Edwards elicited boos and catcalls as he attempted to defend his support for a war that was about to start. The crowd, a few thousand of the party diehards in California, was getting a close look at the men seeking the Democratic nod, and not liking what it saw.

And then Howard Dean walked on stage.

"What I want to know is what in the world so many Democrats are doing supporting the President's unilateral intervention in Iraq?"

That brought loud cheers from the delegates.

"What I want to know is what in the world so many Democrats are doing supporting tax cuts which have bankrupted this country and given us the largest deficit in the history of the United States?"

More cheers. Dean certainly had the crowd's full attention, and he was just getting warmed up.

"What I want to know is why the Congress is fighting over the Patient's Bill of Rights? The Patient's Bill of Rights is a good bill, but not one more person gets health insurance and it's not five cents cheaper. What I want to know is why the Democrats in Congress aren't standing up for us joining every other industrialized country on the face of the earth in having health insurance for every man, woman, and child in America?"

By now, the chants of "Dean! Dean!" had begun and the crowd was on its feet.

"What I want to know is why so many folks in Congress are voting for the President's education bill—the "No School Board Left Standing" bill— the largest unfunded mandate in the history of our educational system?"

And then Dean fed that "red meat" crowd a line borrowed from the late Paul Wellstone which resonated with them.

"I'm Howard Dean, and I'm here to represent the Democratic wing of the Democratic Party."

Dean then blasted both John Kerry and John Edwards for their support of the Iraq War, talked about how he'd balanced the budget in Vermont and how every child under eighteen was covered under Medicaid in Vermont. He then wound up the crowd a bit more.

"We are not going to beat George Bush by voting with the president 85 percent of the time. The only way that we're going to beat George Bush is to say what we mean, to stand up for who we are, to lift up a Democratic agenda against the Republican agenda, because if you do that, the Democratic agenda wins every time."

On a roll and all pumped up by now, Dean raised his voice louder as he closed his speech.

"I want my country back! We want our country back! I'm tired of being divided! I don't want to listen to the fundamentalist preachers anymore! I want America to look like America, where we are all included, hand in hand, walking down. We have a dream. We can only reach the dream if we are all together—black and white, gay and straight, man and woman. America! The Democratic Party!"

The crowd was on its feet, the convention hall shaking from audience pandemonium, the speech serving as liberation of sorts—a vindication for every party activist who had lived through the Democratic Party's "abused puppy" routine the previous two years. They weren't alone in the fight. Not anymore. They had a champion and his name was Howard Dean. The call to arms by Dean was ideologically agnostic, purely partisan. It had to be, because Dean wasn't the liberal candidate his opponents and the press (not to mention Republicans) made him out to be.

Dean's campaign was an altogether new kind of campaign—it wasn't about offering a list of "policy fixes"; it was more about creating a broad-based populism that energized the base by giving it voice in a national forum, and it was about boldly fighting Republicans, not imitating them. Using tools like Meetup.com, his merry band of bloggers, and the relatively new service unions like SEIU and AFCSME Dean built an army of foot soldiers that far outnumbered anything his opponents could muster.

Money talks loud and clear in electoral campaigns, and by June 2003 the party establishment was reeling from Dean's second quarter financial windfall—he had raised $7.6 million. Runner-up John Kerry had raised $5.9 million. But by September, the money war had become an all-out rout, with Dean hauling in $14.8 million to Kerry's $4 million in the third quarter. The rest of the candidates languished in the $3-million range or lower. After the election, when he was asked by CNN's Judy Woodruff *when* he knew Dean had a chance, campaign manager Joe Trippi said: "The end of June 2003, in that unbelievable three or four days when millions came in over the Internet and $829,000 came in on Monday, the FEC deadline day."

That money was all the more remarkable because it was mostly internet-generated small-dollar donations. The Democratic Party had never seen anything like it before. The party, which was struggling to survive because of its gross inability to compete with Republicans on the hard-dollar front (because of McCain-Feingold), was watching a little-known candidate being flooded with exactly the kind of donations needed to build the party.

Dean for America was a fifty-state movement, with over 160,000 people attending decentralized Meetups. Its small-dollar donor base raised $50 million with an average contribution of about $70. Its volunteer ranks were swollen with netroots and grassroots supporters. The nation's two largest unions were working on its behalf.

And instead of embracing this new energized voter-donor community, the Democratic Party establishment geared up to squash it.

THE RESISTANCE

Howard Dean's candidacy had ignited an intraparty battle between outsider agitators and the D.C.-based insider establishment. The Democratic Leadership Council (DLC), an organization that arose in the late 1980s to battle the corrosive interest groups, now represented the epitome of the insider establishment groups—intellectually lazy, stuck in the past, oblivious to the nation's changing political landscape. Still traumatized by the Democratic Party's 1972 and 1984 presidential losses (with George McGovern and Walter Mondale, respectively), the Democrats at the DLC feared that social liberalism and the issue groups promoting it were again killing the party—both by hurting its fundraising among corporate donors and by putting it out of step with an increasingly socially conservative American electorate.

In its early years, the DLC eschewed the remnants of the New Deal in favor of a business-friendly model. It obsessed about the "vital center" on social and economic issues, rejecting the "left" on trade, welfare, and social issues. They battled against the party's entrenched special interest groups, and the Left-Labor axis. Former DLC chairman Bill Clinton was elected president in 1992, and the DLC, which began as a guerilla outsider group in the 1980s, slowly wormed its way to the core of the party establishment in the 1990s—especially as its business-friendly ideology matched up nicely with the party's increasing appetite for large soft-dollar donations. The organization had morphed from fighting entrenched constituency groups to becoming one itself. Meanwhile, the party's grassroots atrophied and were all but dead by the time 2003 rolled around and Dean burst on to the national stage.

As noted earlier, the 2002 campaign finance reform law radically changed the political landscape. Soft-dollar donations were suddenly out of reach, and with the electoral disasters of 2000 and 2002, the DLC and the establishment in D.C. were at a complete loss. The candidates they favored for the 2004 presidential line-up—like Lieberman and Gephardt—were still living in the 1990s, ill-prepared to operate in this new political terrain where energizing Democratic voters is far more important than sucking up to big-money interests.

None of them understood the growth of this new movement or its sheer size, even as it gathered steam, powering the Dean phenomenon. If anything, the Democratic establishment perceived it as a serious threat. The centrist minds at the DLC had a difficult strategic question to answer heading into the Democratic primaries: How could they keep this new populist movement at bay and ensure a beltway-friendly Democratic presidential nominee? The answer was to redefine these outsiders and the Dean campaign as the new incarnation of the party's now-dead 1970s-1990's liberal wing.

The DLC took point position in the battle against Dean. Its leadership—Founder and CEO Al From, President Bruce Reed, and cofounder Will Marshall—focused on the language and rhetoric Dean was using. They decided to log outrageous comments by Dean, anything "really *out there*" and "lefty" that Dean had ever said, all the "real crazy stuff," according to a then-employee of the DLC. But they found no ammunition. In fact, Dean had been praised by the DLC in one of its "Idea of the Week" columns in October 2000.

In one of the DLC's monthly staff meetings, From explained his fears of a Dean candidacy—his angry tone, his borrowing of the Wellstone rhetoric, his "weakness" on national security issues and his opposition to the brewing Iraq War. From believed that Dean's use of Wellstone's "Democratic wing of the Democratic Party" line was directly aimed at Clinton's centrist policies and therefore at the DLC. From took it all as a personal affront, saying that "Dean would undo everything that Clinton had stood for" and put the Democratic Party permanently back into minority status—à la Mondale in 1984. At one point, the normally reserved From pounded the table and said that "the DLC was there to protect the Democratic Party from itself," said a source who was present.

Dean's record in Vermont showed that he was a moderate and that while he was veering left in the primaries, he would most likely run a centrist campaign in the general election if he won the nomination. So the DLC attack plan focused on hitting Dean and defining him early enough in the primary as an unelectable northeasterner who was trotting out the tired, old, failed liberalism of McGovern and Mondale.

The DLC publicly launched its anti-Dean campaign on May 15, 2003, by releasing a memo titled "The Real Soul of the Democratic Party."[65] It was a broadside against party activists, saying, "the great myth of the current cycle is the misguided notion that the hopes and dreams of activists represent the heart and soul of the Democratic Party. Real Democrats are real people, not activist elites." It went without saying, of course, that Dean was one of those *activist elites*. Most famously, the memo declared: "What activists like Dean call the Democratic wing of the Democratic Party is an aberration; the McGovern-Mondale wing, defined principally by weakness abroad and elitist, interest-group liberalism at home." The implications were clear—McGovern and Mondale were the epitome of "unelectable" candidates, both huge losers in their respective presidential contests in 1972 and 1984.

The stoking of the "unelectable" theme by the DLC was born out of frustration from the real lack of substantive problems with Dean's record. No salacious rumors, no big lawsuits, nothing that could dismiss him out of hand. The DLC thus counted on the intense desire by Democrats to unify behind the guy with the best chance to defeat Bush. And it worked. The problem of Dean's electability was picked up and used by anti-Dean pundits on the airwaves, in print, and online. While analyzing a pre–New Hampshire poll showing Dean fading away, pollster John Zogby wrote, "Howard Dean was the man of the year, but that was 2003. In 2004, electability has become the issue and John Kerry has benefited."

The attack included the online circles driving Dean's fundraising, which were a source of constant amusement to the beltway crowd. An unnamed rival consultant mocked Dean Meetups (monthly gatherings of Dean supporters at bars and restaurants all across the country) comparing them to "the bar scene from Star Wars."[66] The usual suspects caricatured Dean supporters as out-of-touch left-wing radicals, or idealists, or "activist elites."

The anti-Dean crusade took a nasty turn in the fall. On November 7, 2003, a mysterious new group called Americans for Jobs and Healthcare ran a series of ads against Dean in Iowa, distorting his record, criticizing him for his positions on trade, Medicare growth, and gun rights, implying that Dean was not a progressive. The worst of the lot zoomed into the eyes of Osama bin Laden on the cover of *Time* magazine while the announcer intoned, "We live in a very dangerous world. And there are those who wake up every morning determined to destroy western civilization. . . . Americans want a president who can face the dangers ahead. But Howard Dean has no military or foreign policy experience. And Howard Dean just cannot compete with George Bush on foreign policy. It's time for Democrats to think about that . . . and think about it now."

While the ads were running, the group refused to reveal the identities of its financial backers. Only after the Iowa caucuses were over did the group file its first financial disclosure records and the truth began to trickle out. The effort was run by a combined team of Kerry and Gephardt loyalists, including several labor unions, and organized by disgraced, corrupt former New Jersey senator Robert Toricelli, who donated $50,000 of the organization's $663,000 budget from his left-over U.S. Senate campaign war chest to the group. A study by the Center for Public Integrity found that the twenty-eight contributors to Americans for Jobs and Health Care had given more than $8.7 million to the Democratic Party in the previous couple of years (including $417,000 to Gephardt).[67] The group's spokesman was former John Kerry press secretary Robert Gibbs; its "custodian of records" and executive director was David Jones, a long-time Gephardt operative. Leo Hindery, Gephardt's national finance co-chair was also a substantial funder. Neither Kerry nor Gephardt has ever answered or explained the despicable tactics of the group; presumably both candidates had "plausible deniability" when asked whether they knew about the effort before it was launched.

Ultimately, Dean collapsed under the weight of the establishment and the other candidate attacks (especially from Gephardt), a hostile media (being fed weekly attacks by Wesley Clark's communications strategist Chris Lehane), a series of gaffes, a shockingly spendthrift campaign, and the quirks of the Iowa caucuses. By the time Dean made his infamous "scream," the disastrous results were already in and Dean had come in a distant third place with 18 percent of the delegates compared to 37.6 percent for John Kerry and 31.8 percent for John Edwards. The scream merely cemented Dean's then inevitable demise.

At the DLC, the day after the Iowa caucus was a joyous one. At a pizza-party celebration, Bruce Reed and Will Marshall were giddy with excitement. So giddy in fact, a partygoer informed us, "they engaged in the dorkiest high-five ever, and an effort toward a chest bump. It was sad." Dean lost in a state where the majority of residents were against the war in Iraq, so the DLC brain trust knew he was done. Marshall, we were told, referred to the Gephardt/Dean blood-bath as a "murder/suicide."

THE RISE OF THE NETROOTS

As technology became increasingly ingrained in the fabric of daily life, it was only natural that politics would find a home in the burgeoning online world. The lack of geographic boundaries made it easy for like-minded individuals to form large-scale communities. And technological advancements made it possible for nontechnical people to take a larger role in organizing and running such communities.

We are both very much a part of this new wave of political activism, and it was Jerome who coined the term "netroots" in 2002 to describe this online grassroots community that has grown dramatically in the past five years. MoveOn.org, launched in 1998 to combat the right-wing effort to destroy then president Bill Clinton, has grown to 3.3 million members. By late November 2005, the top seventy or so liberal blogs, led by Daily Kos, garnered about 60 million page-views every month.

The netroots were instrumental in pushing Dean to the forefront and played a key role in drafting General Wesley Clark into the 2004 presidential race, proving that this small but growing movement was developing some serious political muscle. And by and large, the netroots are bonded not by their allegiance to any single issue, but by their belief that only a broad-based progressivism will save the nation from the destructive influences of the current administration.

The netroots activist, much like the new generation of grassroots activist, is fiercely partisan, fiercely multi-issue, and focused on building a broader movement. It's not an ideological movement— there is actually very little, issue-wise, that unites most modern party activists except, perhaps opposition to the Iraq War (though opposition to the war seems to be uniting the entire country as of late). The days when party "leaders" could hand down edicts from above to be carried out by pliant followers are long gone. We are educated, informed, up on current events, and speak our minds, and therefore are not susceptible to falling in line and goose-stepping to autocratic drummers—inside or outside the movement.

The netroots can be the loudest and strongest proponents of the party when necessary and when they believe in the specific cause, but they can also be the loudest and strongest critics of the party when it makes boneheaded moves.

Take the example of Pennsylvania's Eighth Congressional District race in 2004. When the Republican representative stepped down from his seat in the summer of 2004, political blogs were abuzz. This was a nearly even district that had a progressive candidate already in the running. The blogs jumped on it, creating a bit of hoopla that resulted in around $30,000 being contributed to Virginia "Ginny" Schraeder overnight. The Democratic Congressional Campaign Committee (DCCC), which was used to handpicking its candidates, didn't exactly appreciate the gesture, declining to comment on whether it would support Schraeder.

Tensions built online over the rift and exploded at a "blogger party" ironically sponsored by the DCCC at the July 2004 Democratic National Convention in Boston. Then DCCC executive director Jim Bonham approached Markos as the crowd was dispersing for the evening. In front of maybe two dozen people, Bonham screamed demands that Markos fall in line, "You can raise $30,000? We can raise $30 million!" A week or so later, Bonham proudly proclaimed to shocked DCCC staffers, "That'll show the bloggers that I'm not afraid of Markos!" according to a DCCC staffer present at the meeting.

As much as bloggers and the netroots mobilized leading up to the 2004 elections, the night of November 2 was a downer for them, as it was for half the country. But in the weeks following the election, something phenomenal and new happened. While a lot of loyal Democrats went into depression and slunk away to lick their wounds, the netroots became more energized.

It's hard to believe now, but this was a time that know-nothing

pundits predicted the demise of the netroots and Democratic consultants dreamed of business-as-usual. But the netroots remained moti-
vated, engaged, and ready to clean house of the losers who gave us the
2004 debacle. This sentiment—of fixing the problems that led us to
lose the election—was expressed in a variety of ways online, but none
did it as bluntly as Eli Pariser of MoveOn PAC, who sent his now-leg-
endary and highly controversial e-mail about the Democratic Party to
the group's supporters on December 9, 2004. "For years, the party has
been led by elite Washington insiders who are closer to corporate lobbyists than they are to the Democratic base," Pariser wrote. "But we
can't afford four more years of leadership by a consulting class of professional election losers. . . . In the last year, grass-roots contributors
like us gave more than $300 million to the Kerry campaign and the
DNC, and proved that the party doesn't need corporate cash to be
competitive. Now it's our party: we bought it, we own it, and we're
going to take it back."

As brazen as Pariser's note was, it foreshadowed a major change at
the DNC. Bloggers like us were already plotting to push for a "reform
candidate" to take over as party chairman—a clarion call picked up
by party activists around the country the day after the election,
November 3.

It was obvious that Terry McAuliffe, the former Clinton fundraiser-
in-chief, was finished as DNC Chairman. His record fundraising
hadn't been enough to mask the electoral losses suffered by the party
under his helm, and he declared he wouldn't run for reelection. John
Kerry, under delusions that he was still in charge of the party (a courtesy always given presidential nominees), imperially signaled that
Iowa Governor Tom Vilsack should take the helm. Senate Minority
Leader Harry Reid and House Minority Leader Nancy Pelosi
promptly lined up behind Vilsack. It seemed to be business as usual—
the leaders calling the shots, handpicking candidates for office and
everyone else nodding in agreement.

But this time, the party got a reality check from the netroots.

Democratic activists from across the new reform movement snorted in derision at the Vilsack nomination, basically told Kerry to shove it, and pointed the uninspiring Vilsack, who wasn't even going to take on the position full-time, to the door. Realizing that he wasn't going to be appointed by fiat, Vilsack bowed out of the race in November, at the first sign of conflict. Kerry then tried to get former New Hampshire governor Jeanne Shaheen into the race, but she demurred. That was the end of Kerry's embarrassing efforts to play kingmaker.

The netroots backed the effort to draft Howard Dean into the race, while also lending a friendly hand to reform candidates like Simon Rosenberg, president of the New Democrat Network. The bloggers, just about the only source of regular information on the DNC chairman race, became a go-to source for news by party enthusiasts and insiders. And we trained our guns on anyone in the way of the reform candidates.

MyDD.com became a clearinghouse for news, leaks, and other inside information on the chairman's race, capped by Jerome's weekly candidate rankings. Jerome, along with blogger Matt Stoller from BOP News & MyDD, and Joe Trippi, who was blogging for MSNBC, attended the first big event of the race in Orlando, Florida—a meeting of Democratic state party chairs. The trio was tossed out of the convention hall for blogging the event. They then blogged their ejection and encouraged party grassroots activists to attend the four regional events to influence DNC members. Meanwhile, the netroots and bloggers focused their resources on the opposing candidates.

First up was Leo Hindery, a big-money donor to the Democratic Party and various interest groups, a business-friendly Democrat that was backed by McAuliffe, Gephardt, and Tom Daschle. We targeted him on our blogs (Daily Kos and MyDD) for his role in corporate scandals and—most damaging—for being one of the chief funders of that infamous Osama/Dean ad in Iowa, providing $100,000 of a total $663,000 budget for the group sponsoring those ads. En route to the Orlando event via his private jet, Hindery abruptly turned around after learning from aides that the blogs had destroyed his chances and revealed his anti-Dean role.

In similar fashion the bloggers took out each one of the status-quo candidates in the race. Ousted congressman Martin Frost of Texas was finished after blogger Anna Brosovic of Annatopia.com dug up 2004 campaign ads with Frost cozying up to George Bush. Declaring that "Frost must be stopped," Anna wrote, "the bottom line is that Martin was running to save himself, and he did it at the expense of the Democrats in north Texas."[68] Another former congressman, Tim Roemer of Indiana, who seemed to have the support of Pelosi and Reid, was taken on by bloggers Chris Bowers and Kevin Drum for positions that seemed to advocate for the privatization of Social Security and making abortion illegal, and by blogger Josh Marshall for Roemer's vote against Clinton's economic plan in 1993. There was also the not-so-minor detail that Roemer was on the board of the right-wing, Scaife-funded Mercatus Center at George Mason University, which made his progressive credentials a bit suspect. While on ABC's *This Week*, Roemer had to confront the issue of the bloggers' influence on the Democratic Party, when George Stephanopoulos gently informed him that the progressive base of the Democratic Party is "taking their cues from these Web logs, the blogs that are, you know, engaged in this debate."[69]

Ultimately, no blogger had a vote in the race, a privilege given to 447 DNC members, mostly from outside D.C. Activists lobbied these members mercilessly. Those holding positions in the DNC were notified that the grassroots was watching. At each of the regional events, Dean supporters gathered in unprecedented numbers for what used to be nonevents in years past.

Of course, Dean also won a great deal of backing from DNC members based on good ol' fashioned politicking of his own—telling them some of what they wanted to hear and promising large-scale help to the state parties (which alone represented over half the votes). But his task was made far easier when the field was cleared of most of his rivals, with a little help from bloggers and the netroots. And while hapless establishment Democrats blathered on about having Dean become DNC chair "over their dead body" and desperately sought a candidate that could survive the withering attacks from the bloggers, Dean quietly built his winning coalition. In the end, the threat of a contested chairman's race vanished as one by one, the rest of the candidates bowed to the inevitability of Dean's imminent victory.

On February 12, 2005, Howard Dean was elected chairman of the Democratic National Committee on a voice vote without a single dissenter. Among other things, Dean told the Democrats that day: "This party's strength does not come from consultants down, it comes from the grassroots up."

Dean's victory, as exciting as it may have been for many party activists, was actually bigger than Howard Dean. It was a message to the D.C. establishment that they no longer had total control over the direction of the Democratic Party. As Ryan Lizza noted in his article about the DNC chairman race in the February 14, 2005, issue of *The New Republic*, "the real story of the race is the diffusion of power away from Washington and to new people and entities that have rushed to fill the power vacuum at the top of the party." As blogger Chris Bowers declared, "I can barely believe it. It looks like we finally won something. Outside becomes inside."

Dean was the first to break through and get inside. He won't be the last.

INSIDE THE GATE

"Some of you in the Democratic National Committee may see us as the barbarians at the gate. Some of us see ourselves as the cavalry. The truth is, we're fresh horses."
—Activist Miles Kurland, speaking at the DNC Western Regional Caucus in Sacramento, January 2005

We landed in Helena, Montana, late at night in July 2005, and picked up the local daily, the *Helena Independent Record*, after getting to our hotel. On the front page was a picture of Montana governor Brian Schweitzer, on a Harley at a hog rally, with his bolo tie and his cowboy hat. The gruff bikers were raising money for charity, and Schweitzer was obviously having fun hanging with them. Above the photo, a headline blared, "State Posts $300M Surplus." The next morning, we found Schweitzer in his office, which is lined with moccasins and other Native American paraphernalia given him by Indian tribes and a framed picture of Montana One (a turboprop) parked in front of Air Force One (a 747 jumbo jet). Schweitzer pulled out a copy of that same newspaper, pointed to the front page and asked us, "Did you see this? Do you know what this is?" We shrugged. He answered with a smile, "Re-election."

Harleys and massive budget surpluses may help his re-election chances, but Schweitzer has already transformed the Montana political landscape and brought national attention to this sprawling state. A rancher and a businessman, Schweitzer had no political experience before he nearly ousted incumbent Republican Sen. Conrad Burns in 2000 (Schweitzer lost 51-47). Four years later, campaigning on a platform of environmental conservation, corruption-busting, and economic populism, Schweitzer won a tough gubernatorial race 50-46 against his Republican opponent, Secretary of State Bob Brown. Schweitzer also had long coattails, helping elect Democrats to four of the five statewide offices and recapturing both houses of the state legislature. All this in Montana, where Bush beat Kerry 59-39 the same year and where the congressional delegation consists of two ultraright Republicans (Burns and Representative Denny Rehberg) and a conservative Democrat (Senator Max Baucus).

Because of its Republican leanings, Montana is like many other states that national Democrats have long abandoned as not winnable, focusing instead on an increasingly shrinking number of "swing states." Yet Schweitzer and company have proven that sincere, populist Democrats can win anywhere.

While the experience in Montana and similar state legislative gains in Colorado in 2004 hint at a Democratic revival in the libertarian-leaning Mountain West, the South poses a different challenge altogether. If the Democrats are going to contest in every district and every state of the nation, as they should, it's the South that's going to prove the toughest nut to crack. The entire Republican ascendancy has pivoted on winning the hearts and minds of southern white voters.

Virginia, which hasn't voted for a Democratic president since Lyndon Johnson in 1964, is a revealing example of how Democrats can make inroads in the South. In 2000, Republicans controlled both houses in the legislature and every statewide office, the same year that Bush beat Gore by 8 percentage points in the state and Republican George Allen knocked off the sitting Democratic Senator, Chuck Robb. Republicans, having made gains in every election since 1974, took over the Virginia House of Delegates with a super majority in 2001.

It was clearly a red state and getting redder when Democrat Mark Warner ran for governor in Virginia.* During his 2001 campaign, Warner reached out to Virginians in rural communities—to people who hadn't voted for a Democrat in a long, long time. "We won because we built a new coalition of Virginians," Warner explained in a May 31, 2003, speech to a gathering of Democrats in Jackson, Mississippi. "We did that by laying out a message that focused on meeting the needs of an information-age economy—a message that stressed economic opportunity, educational opportunities, and fiscal responsibility. And then we said something a lot of people had never thought of—you can like NASCAR, you can like hunting, you can like bluegrass music, and you can still vote for a Democrat. We did all this because we recognized that if you're going to offer people economic hope, you can't spend all your time talking about the same old social issues that have divided us for too long. You can't move forward if every discussion is about abortion and guns."

If Democrats are going to win back the White House, Warner says, it's going to happen because Democrats "reclaim rural America," and not cede the higher moral ground to Republicans. "I'll put our moral values up against the other side's any day. I'll take 'We're all in this together' over 'You're on your own' any day. I think most Americans would, if we put the choice to them.[70] But if we want to get a fair hearing on the bread-and-butter issues—health, education, the economy—then we've got to start acting like the cultural issues, what some people are calling the 'moral values' issues, really count. Not just politically. We're the party that says everyone counts. . . . But here's the catch. We can't apply these principles with respect to race and gender—and then take a pass on region or religion. We've never believed that some people count and some people don't. So we need to stop acting that way. That's not who we are, and we've got to make that clear."

---

* Jerome works as a strategic advisor with Forward Together PAC, which is chaired by Governor Mark Warner.

Warner made that clear and he won. He not only beat Attorney General Mark Earley 52 to 47 percent, but in the process, made it perfectly fine and respectable to vote Democratic in Virginia. Then he went on to deliver on his agenda, enacting progressive changes to education funding and tax reform, driving antitax ideologues like Grover Norquist crazy. In fact, Warner has been so popular and successful that near the end of his term, in October 2005, a *Washington Post* poll showed him with 80 percent approval ratings, unheard of for a governor in Virginia, Democrat or Republican. And while term-limited, (Virginia has a one-term limit) he could take heart in the fact that succeeding him was another Democrat, Lieutenant Governor Tim Kaine, who handily won the gubernatorial contest 52 to 46 percent over a Republican, Attorney General Jerry Kilgore. And down-ticket, for the first time since 1943, Virginia Democrats picked up seats in the House for the second consecutive election cycle.

The Democratic Party is in the upswing in the Mountain West and the South, in places like Montana and Virginia, because Democrats there have made a serious effort to compete for votes everywhere, rather than make a nominal effort to be an "also-ran" outside the Democratic-density areas. As Warner asks, how many more times will the Democrats run presidential campaigns where they abandon thirty-something southern and western states and "launch a national campaign that goes after sixteen states and then hope that we can hit a triple bank shot to get to that seventeenth state?"

In the 1992 and the 1996 presidential elections, with three candidates in the race, as many as thirty states were viewed as competitive battleground contests up through election day. In 2000, that number dropped to just seventeen by election day. In 2004, the number of contested states early in the presidential contest stood at eighteen, and was whittled down to about eight by election day.

This strategy—or more accurately this obsession—that the Democratic establishment in D.C. has with narrowing electoral campaigns to ever shrinking "swing states" is self-defeating. It doesn't build any new converts to the party, it makes it easier for the Republicans to walk away with huge chunks of the country unchallenged, and it starves the Democratic Parties in those "red" states. But don't tell that to Bob Shrum, the über-consultant who lost eight presidential campaigns so far and won zero. Asked by writer Ben Smith in the November 21, 2005, issue of the *New York Observer* whether he had any regrets about his work on Kerry's campaign, Shrum responded that had he believed Florida would go for Bush so strongly, "the campaign would have sent more resources—including Mr. Kerry—to Ohio." One can only hope that Bob Shrum won't be back in 2008 to run one more Democratic candidate into the ground with his overpriced expertise and a three-state strategy.

But this isn't just a presidential-year malaise for Democrats—it happens every election cycle in the congressional races.

CHALLENGE EVERY REPUBLICAN

Reform-minded activists feuded for years with the Democratic Congressional Campaign Committee (DCCC) regarding its selective targeting of U.S. House races. Ever since losing the majority in 1994, the DCCC has targeted about thirty or so races every two years, just enough by its calculations to provide a simple majority—and has abandoned Democrats in all the other races. The Committee has argued that it simply doesn't have the money and resources to fight on a broader front, and it's true—the DCCC was outspent by its Republican counterpart $84 million to $32 million in the 2004 cycle. Yet, the party must have a better approach than narrowing its efforts to the districts it sees as "winnable"—that may serve the short-term interest of trying for a slim majority in the House, but it completely ignores the long-term interest of building a wider, nationwide base for the party. But even in the short term, that strategy hurts Democrats.

For example, in 2004, the DCCC ignored fourteen of the seventy-two House districts in four key "battleground" states (Arizona, Florida, Pennsylvania, and Virginia), according to fundraising research done by Project 90, an organization built by political consultant Walter Ludwig to encourage long-shot challengers. If the DCCC had adopted a "challenge every Republican" strategy and fielded competitive candidates in those fourteen districts, it would have certainly netted a few hundred—or a few thousand—more Democratic votes in each district, helping the top of the ticket, especially John Kerry. In the top-tier battleground state of Florida, Democrats failed to even field a candidate in six congressional districts, according to DCPoliticalReport.com.

Overall, Democrats failed to field a candidate to challenge over 15 percent of Republican incumbents in the U.S. House in 2004. This hurts the chances of Democrats to retake the presidency and the Senate, and also hurts Democrats running for state and local offices—governor, state legislature, county executive, among others.

As blogger Chris Bowers of MyDD noted on November 5, 2004:

> Failing to challenge your opponent's message in an area is damaging to your message in that area in the future. Failing to provide a choice to those willing to support you—and there are always tens of thousands willing to support you in any congressional district—sends a message that you do not represent or care about those people. Even worse, failing to challenge an incumbent sends a message that you are afraid of your own beliefs and that you are not working to make this country a better democracy.
>
> Running a candidate in each of these districts would also have helped to identify Democratic activists in each of these districts. Identifying, encouraging, and assisting potential

Dem activists throughout the entire country would help to strengthen the Party, both now and in future election cycles. These are the people who can help to bring the Democratic message to every corner of the country.[71]

Furthermore, challenging Republicans in "deep red" districts forces Republican incumbents to spend a great deal of time and money defending their seats instead of campaigning for other Republicans and donating to their campaigns. Project 90 found that "between 2000–2004, Democrats failed to compete or barely challenge in over a quarter of U.S. House races, and the Republican incumbents in those districts contributed over $60 [million] to their colleagues in closer races."

Beltway political analyst Stuart Rothenberg mocked Bowers in the January 27, 2005, edition of *Roll Call* as an example of "how clueless some bloggers really are about politics" for urging a wider electoral battlefield, but it's not just bloggers urging an aggressive and broad challenge to congressional Republicans. Even former U.S. representative Martin Frost, a two-time chair of the DCCC whom we opposed for the DNC chair, has come to understand the importance of competing in all fifty states. As he wrote on September 12, 2005, on FoxNews.com:

Ever since losing the House and Senate in 1994, Democrats have narrowed rather than expanded the playing field. The theory was to concentrate resources in those races where we had the best chance to win. That strategy was successful for House Democrats in 1996 and 1998 when we picked up a total of fourteen seats despite being badly outspent by Republicans. But it didn't get us back into the majority and it led to a stalemate in the next three elections. Senate Democrats picked up a few seats last time around, but ultimately were dealt a significant loss in 2004.

It's now time to shoot the moon. Recruit and file everywhere and then late in the cycle decide which races present
the best opportunities. Be prepared to win some seats that
you don't deserve because the "force is with you."

A look at two U.S. House contests in 2004—one in Texas, the
other in Colorado—shows the potential gains in challenging even
those seemingly invincible Republicans. It wasn't the DCCC that
chose to engage in these races; it was the netroots who took up the
fight.

The blogger effort on behalf of Richard Morrison was particularly
seen as a fool's errand by the DCCC. Morrison was a political nobody
going up against House Majority Leader Tom DeLay of Texas, the
second most powerful Republican in the House, who had retained his
seat in 2002 with a solid 63 percent of the vote. Over the summer, netroots consultant Nathan Wilcox raised Morrison's profile among the
bloggers while the national party completely ignored the insurgent.
With an aggressive grassroots effort, Morrison kept DeLay focused on
winning his district for the first time since DeLay's initial campaign
back in 1984, forcing DeLay to raise more funds to defend his seat,
rather than raise funds and campaign on behalf of other Republicans
in tight districts. Morrison spent $685,935, just a little more than *one-
fifth* of Delay's $3.1 million in a heavily Republican district.[72] And yet,
Delay only managed a remarkably low 55 percent of the vote.

In Colorado's Fourth Congressional District, which hasn't elected a
Democrat since 1972, Congresswoman Marilyn Musgrave is well
known for her singular obsession with homosexuality during her
career as a state legislator; in the U.S. House, her claim to fame so far
has been in leading the effort to pass the antigay marriage amendment. In 2004, the DCCC wrote off the district since Stan
Matsunaka had lost to Musgrave in 2002 by 13 percentage points
despite a large DCCC investment.

Bloggers took up Matsunaka's cause and raised almost $100,000 for his race. After Matsunaka gained some momentum, the Colorado-based 527 group, Colorado Families First, did some heavy lifting, spending about $850,000 in airing attack ads against Musgrave. Bobby Clark, fresh from working on Dean's campaign, worked the blogosphere network with inside scoops from Colorado. Musgrave, who had likely planned to campaign and fund other antigay candidates, was in the fight of her life. She ended up blowing through her entire $3.3 million campaign war chest, about four times Matsunaka's expenditures of $868,439. The National Republican Congressional Committee came to Musgrave's rescue with another $2 million, according to campaign filings. At the end of election day, Musgrave won, but by a 51-45 margin, the closest in the district since 1974. There were two tangible benefits from this race being contested seriously by a Democrat: the vote turnout undoubtedly helped Ken Salazar win his tight U.S. Senate race—one of only two Democrats (Barack Obama of Illinois was the other) to flip Senate seats from Republican to Democrat in 2004, and the House race cost Republicans $5 million, a lot of which would have otherwise gone to help Republicans in other hotly contested races.

The 2004 results in the House districts in Texas and Colorado seem to have drawn the attention of the DCCC. There are indications that it will be engaged more heavily in those districts, come 2006. Bloggers also backed candidates that bombed, but that risk was factored into their efforts—you provide a little seed money to a lot of campaigns, and several unexpectedly close races will arise.

The netroots have been particularly successful in special elections, when they can focus the entire nationwide network on a single race. During 2004, they provided assists to two special-election wins, powering Democrats to victory in heavily conservative congressional districts in Kentucky and South Dakota. In Kentucky, Ben Chandler created a stir when a Blogads campaign costing $2,000 netted over

$80,000 for the February 2004 race in the waning days. In South Dakota, Stephanie Herseth garnered a great deal of national attention and netroots fundraising en route to a narrow victory in June 2004.

The 2005 special election in Ohio's Second District was a great example of why Democrats should take on all districts, no matter how heavily Republican they swing. Bush won the district with 64 percent of the vote in 2004 and no Democrat had won the district since 1974. So when the seat opened up April 29, 2005, triggering a special election, the D.C. Democratic political establishment yawned and planned on surrendering the seat without a fight. Republicans staged a bitter primary, figuring the winner would waltz into office against weak or nonexistent Democratic opposition.

But online Democratic activists, ready to get over the 2004 losses, saw a chance to rejoin the fight with the Republicans. They were especially excited about the Democratic candidate who stepped into the race. It was Paul Hackett, a relative neophyte, politically speaking. A personal-injury lawyer who had served on the city council of Milford, Ohio, from 1995–98, he had recently returned from a seven-month tour of duty in the Iraq War as a Marine Corps reservist. He was an outspoken Democrat, a telegenic and articulate speaker who minced no words (he called Bush a "chickenhawk" and the "greatest threat to America"), he opposed drilling in the Arctic National Wildlife Refuge in Alaska, he was pro-choice on abortion, and generally speaking, he came across to voters as a genuine straight-shooter, a sincere man, an un-politician. He faced Jean Schmidt, whom he promptly labeled a "rubber stamp" for Bush and his conservative cohorts.

A group of bloggers in Ohio, led by Ann Driscoll's diary postings on MyDD, the OH-02 blog, and Tim Tagaris of Representative Sherrod Brown's GrowOhio.org blog, took up Hackett's cause and were quickly joined by SwingStateProject.com's Bob Brigham and ActBlue.com's Matt DeBergalis. Soon the regulars at Daily Kos and MyDD were onto the race, followed by the folks over at Democracy for America (the organization founded by Howard Dean in the wake of his presidential primary loss). These online activists raised money, parried Republican smear attacks on Hackett, generated volunteers, performed opposition research, and created a nationwide (online) blogswarm in a race otherwise invisible in the traditional media and D.C. political establishment. When a writer from *Mother Jones* magazine visited Hackett for an interview, Hackett introduced the writer to the "insurgents," bloggers that arrived from around the country, including DeBergalis and Brigham, and Tagaris from Ohio. The article in the November/December 2005 issue said: "The insurgents delivered big time: They out-fundraised the national Democratic Party, hauling in some $500,000 of the campaign's $850,000 total, with nearly 9,000 people giving an average of $50 each. In a show of blogforce on the campaign's last day, Swing State Project put out the word at 10:30 a.m. that Hackett needed $30,000 for get-out-the-vote operations. Six hours later, $60,000 had poured in and Brigham had to tell people to stop giving."

When election day (August 2, 2005) was over, Hackett had come shockingly close—he lost by a mere 3.5 percent. The National Journal 's Charlie Cook called the narrow margin of victory "a very serious warning sign for Ohio Republicans that something is very, very wrong." [73]

For its part, the DCCC was the "Johnny-come-lately" to the campaign. And while it dropped $200,000 into the race, it did so only after the Republican Party had gotten involved, and too late in the game. In its defense after the election, the DCCC meekly claimed it had been "monitoring" the race closely and didn't want to engage too early for fear it would draw fire (and money) from the NRCC too soon. They figured early involvement would've tipped off Republicans that the race was getting closer, so they did nothing but "wait and observe," a senior DCCC official told us after the race.

While their excuses were lame, and while their lack of involvement generated a great deal of netroots hostility, there was a silver lining to their inaction—without their money to wield as a cudgel, Hackett was spared the curse of the D.C. beltway consultants. Had they parachuted into the race they would've urged Hackett to tone down his Iraq stance, defanged him, stripped him of all personality, and delivered a milquetoast candidate to voters. Instead, we got the candidate we had been urging for so long—fearless, bold, unafraid of taking the battle to Republicans, no matter how conservative the district. There he was, in one of the reddest of the red House districts in the nation, and when he's asked about the prospects of gay marriage, he says: "Gay marriage—who the hell cares? If you're gay you're gay—more power to you. What you want is to be treated fairly by the law and any American who doesn't think that should be the case is, frankly, un-American."

Heading into the 2006 midterms, former Republican House Speaker Newt Gingrich called the race result a "wake-up call to Republicans."[74] And while Jean Schmidt limped across the finish line on election day, she was so bloodied in the campaign that she is a top target not just of Democrats in 2006, but also members of her own party already gearing up for a primary challenge.

After races like Matsunaka's and Morrison's in 2004 and Hackett's near miss in 2005, the DCCC is showing signs of having seen the light. By November 2005, DCCC executive director John Lapp and their blogger, Jesse Lee, responded to the netroots requests by posting a web page with information on all House seats.

Perhaps the DCCC—as it argues—is not able to field a strong candidate and campaign in every House race, but it does have the resources and funds to jump on board with one that "gets hot" from netroots and grassroots activism (as they did with Hackett). And it makes financial sense to challenge every Republican incumbent. If

Republicans think there's a chance they could be "Hacketted" and the DCCC might swoop in, it will spread their resources thinner as they spend more time and money on defending their seats. Money spent on "hopeless" candidates is not money wasted, it's leverage gained.

No matter how you look at it, challenging Republicans in all races and all geographic areas is a good idea—it builds the Democratic Party's brand, it exhausts the Republicans' resources and it sows the seeds for future Democratic wins.

THE STATE TRENCHES

Fred Barnes, the executive editor of The Weekly Standard, penned a December 31, 2004, commentary in the Wall Street Journal entitled "The Incredible Shrinking Dems," in which he touted the dominance of Republicans. "There's another measure of Republican (and Bush) success in 2004. For the first time in more than a century, a Republican president won re-election as his party improved its hold on the House and Senate while increasing its majority of governorships (28 now) and maintaining control of a plurality of state legislatures (20). At the same time, Republicans held a majority of state legislators—a feat they initially achieved in 2002 after a half-century in the minority."

Here's what that propagandist piece conveniently ignored: Republicans have lost governor seats since 2000, and Democrats improved their control of state legislatures from seventeen to twenty since 2000. While Republicans did have a majority of state legislators in 2002, contrary to what Barnes wrote, Republicans lost that majority in 2004, as Democrats gained state legislative seats nationwide and retook the majority 3,661 to 3,653, according to the Democratic Legislative Campaign Committee (DLCC).[75] In fact, despite Barnes' sloppy boasts, Republicans also lost their control of a plurality of state legislatures in 2004, thanks to places like Montana, where Democrats took control.

It's at the state level, looking at those legislative races, that we can find a roadmap to future Democratic success. After visiting with Schweitzer in Helena, Montana, we drove about 170 miles north to a dilapidated and dying town called Big Sandy, with a population of about 150. Its one-block "downtown" had about five viable businesses; at least three of them with "for sale" signs on their windows. More "for sale" signs—some faded with age—adorned empty storefronts. We headed another 10 miles or so out of town before finding the farm of Jon Tester, organic farmer and president of the Montana State Senate. He wasn't in his house when we drove up, so we headed out to the field to find him. Hundreds of grasshoppers jumped out of our path as we walked toward his combine, where he was shucking organic lentils for local consumption and, since it was a good harvest, for Whole Foods nationwide. His clothes were dirty, his face dusty, and his hands calloused. His left hand is missing its three middle fingers—the result of a meat-grinder accident. Tester isn't the sort of person one finds in politics, but Montana's low-cost campaigns (maximum donations allowed are $130), ensure that state politicians tend to be ordinary people more than the rich. And Tester, one such citizen legislator, is a Democratic politician in a district that's over 60 percent Republican. We wanted to know how he did it.

"We went door-to-door five times throughout the district," Tester said, in a refrain echoed by several Montana Democratic legislators we talked with. It was a simple idea—people will cross party lines to vote Democratic if they see and meet a genuine, authentic person, not a packaged, scripted, professional politician.

If there was a winning universal message, it was a standing-up-for-the-underdog populism, the same kind we'd observed in Schweitzer. David Sirota, an advisor to Schweitzer, discussed this theme in the December 2004 edition of the *Washington Monthly*.

"[O]ur first television ads had struck this chord, featuring Schweitzer talking about his small business experience and the need to grow Montana's economy, which has the lowest wages in America," Sirota wrote. "[Schweitzer] seamlessly turned questions about taxation into opportunities to argue that big-box companies like Wal-Mart should pay their fair share and shouldn't be allowed to run roughshod over local business."

It is a message that surprises and resonates in heavily Republican districts where Democrats haven't really contested elections. Partly because of the absence of a Democratic voice, the Republicans have been able to portray them as people who will take away your guns or squander your tax dollars. These portrayals have gone unchallenged for so long that the distorted stereotype endures. And when a candidate like Tester comes along, people are pleasantly surprised to see a Democrat who is normal, sane, and rational and who relates to their concerns well because he is one of them.

Tester is not a political animal, and if he can resist the corrupting whispers of the consultant class and surround himself with the right people—who will let him be himself—he'll go far. Tester hasn't just led a resurgence of Democrats in the state legislature, he is now aiming for Washington, D.C. In May 2005 he announced that he will challenge incumbent Republican senator Conrad Burns in 2006.

Candidates like Tester can help spearhead the people-powered politics that will leave the Democratic establishment in D.C. with no other option than to join the parade. According to the DLCC, twenty of the thirty-six states where district lines will be redrawn in 2010 are within four seats of switching party control. If the Democrats are going to regain power, change is more likely to come from the state and local end than from the party's central command in D.C. And for the new movement populists, taking over the state parties is a good place to start.

TAKING OVER

Howard Dean's ascension to chair of the DNC was a good first step—after all, during his campaign for the chairmanship Dean had embraced a favorite theme of the political blogosphere—to compete in all fifty states. During his first nine months in 2005, Dean had already earned rave reviews from previously skeptical red-state Democrats by following through on promises to help rebuild local parties. The DNC was on pace to put three paid staffers in each state by the end of 2005, and Dean has been aggressively traveling the country raising money not just for the DNC, as past chairmen have done, but for the state parties as well.

Speaking to the National Association of Latino Elected and Appointed Officials in San Juan, Puerto Rico, Dean made clear the new DNC outlook: "As I've said all along, our strategy for victory is a simple one. Show up. Not just in a battleground state. Not just in eighteen of fifty states. Not just show up in blue areas, and not just show up around election time. Show up in every state, in every election, in every community. . . ."

Dean wasn't the only reform-driven takeover of a Democratic Party in 2005. There are reports of grassroots overthrows coming out of states like Oregon and Arkansas. We headed down to North Carolina to get the scoop on another such victory.

"It's good shrimp by the way, and you can quote me on that," said the youthful Jerry Meek, the new chair of the North Carolina Democratic Party, sitting across from us at the 42nd Street Oyster Bar in Raleigh. We're both vegetarians, so we didn't care one way or the other about the shrimp, but Meek had a great story to tell.

Meek had won an upset victory in early 2005 over Ed Turlington, the former state cochairman of local-boy John Edwards' presidential campaign with John Kerry. Turlington not only had Edwards' and the state's entire congressional delegation's blessing to become state party chairman, but also the governor's, the state legislative leaders', and all but one statewide elected official. "Pretty much every single elected Democrat in North Carolina supported my opponent," Meek told us. Yet he won by bringing together a coalition of party activists that had been ignored.

"It was a weird mixture. It was part conservative, rural, and part very liberal urban progressive, and both of them felt the state party had excluded them," Meek said. "The rural people felt like the state party was the party that just invested in the urban areas and had an interest in the urban areas. The urban progressives felt like the state party they ignored them because of their philosophical perspective on politics."

And echoing the same sentiment we find in most components of the new movement, Meek was more interested in building a big tent party than in ideology. "I put together really two coalitions that ordinarily could not coexist in the same room, which made it tricky because during the campaign I never talked about issues—I never talked about whether I'm liberal or moderate or conservative. I just talked about the insiders versus the outsiders. I talked about the need to have a party that embraced everybody and that included people in the decision-making process. And that's what both sides were looking for. And they came together and created a majority."

When the 520 committee members came together to vote, the establishment had pulled in former sixteen-year Democrat governor Jim Hunt (a living legend in North Carolina) to work the room before the vote, and then give the speech to nominate Turlington. Nevertheless, Meek went on to win the chairmanship by twenty-nine votes. It was a stunning victory for the grassroots political movement in the state. The party, Meek told us, had become too reliant on television and radio ads, on paid door-to-door canvassing at election time. "We really lost our volunteer base and the volunteer network that we need to win." Meek's election was about reversing that trend in North

Carolina. "There are people out there to recruit that are willing to get involved."

Meek's example speaks volumes about the new people-powered movement. It's about democratizing America, starting at the local level. For progressives looking to bring the movement fully into the Democratic Party, perhaps the next best move will be to take over the party structure within each state. With Dean at the helm, we would argue that the DNC should also be providing the online organizing tools for local involvement. There is no reason, for instance, why the DNC cannot put detailed information online about every local party election, about every electoral race down to the local level, in the same way that the DCCC has begun to post information about congressional races.

The bloggers and netroots can help organize local activists, as can groups like MoveOn and Democracy For America. When we mentioned this to MoveOn co-founder Wes Boyd, his eyes lit up as he saw the possibility of sending out geo-targeted emails by zip code announcing local Democratic Party precinct and state party elections. Moveon.org has a list of more than 3 million progressive activists nationwide with significant presences in almost every state (West Virginia, for example, has 10,000 members according to MoveOn's Tom Mattzie). The progressive blogosphere has millions of readers in every corner of the nation. A coordinated effort by the netroots and grassroots movement with the blogs working alongside organizations like MoveOn and Democracy for America could help democratize and reform Democratic Party committees at the state and local level.

PEOPLE-POWERED POLITICS

We are at the beginning of a comprehensive reformation of the Democratic Party—driven by committed progressive outsiders.

Online activism on a nationwide level, coupled with offline activists at the local level, à la Meek, can provide the formula for a quiet, bloodless coup that can take control of the party. Money and mobilization are the two key elements of all political activity, and if the netroots have their way, the financial backbone of the Democratic Party will be regular people.

It's been argued that the history of political realignments is best explained by following the money.[76] The bankers and large-dollar donors have held the purse strings of politicians for ages. As recently as the 2000 elections, the Democratic Party relied upon millions in donations from a few individuals. And as we explained earlier, campaign finance reform in 2002 put an end to that, capping the donation amount to candidates and party organizations at $2,000 from each person (with small increases every cycle—it will be $2,100 for 2006).

In the influential 1986 book *Right Turn: The Decline of the Democrats and the Future of American Politics*, Thomas Ferguson and Joel Rogers argued that the nation would continue drifting politically rightward until politics became people-funded and people-powered, until a new mass political movement worked to counter the financial and organizational clout of the Right. "To reverse the right turn of America and the Democrats, it would take investors that were pouring millions of dollars and person-hours into political organizing at all levels," they wrote. "Vast amounts of time and effort would be required to mobilize this generalized sentiment. . . . A new set of political organizations would have to be created. Mechanisms to reach the vast number of nonvoters would be required."

The authors, at the time they wrote their book, had no idea where this new movement would come from. Labor? Even then labor was already in steep decline. Community organizations? Not enough financial clout. The press? They were already being intimidated in the late 1980s. The authors concluded that "if labor, community groups, and the press are currently improbable vehicles for a new mass political movement, it is hard to think of anyone else who might stand in for them."

Of course, Ferguson and Rogers could not have anticipated the advent of the online world and the hundreds of thousands of small donors that propel the new movement.

Similarly in 1980, author Harry Boyte of *The Backyard Revolution: Understanding the New Citizen Movement* saw the need for "organizing-training centers" that would "reach across different groups and networks, able to infuse the movement with vision, coordinate its campaigns, and spread its messages to hidden recesses of society. What such organizing centers might look like for the citizen revolt can only be sketched in general outline, but it is a major question for coming years."

Those organizing networks now exist through online efforts of the netroots and the blogosphere. In previous decades, mobilization was measured through mass protest and marches. Now, the politics of protest activism are, in large part, dead. Once huge media events, the big-march-in-D.C. model of activism is a big media bore. And if the media doesn't cover an event, does it really happen?

If political activism is geared toward changing opinions and attitudes, then action should be aimed toward reaching as many people as possible. Forwarding e-mails are a powerful activism tool—the Flash-based JibJab satirical web videos were e-mail-forwarded to tens of millions of people. Sinclair Broadcasting, whose ultraright owners sought to air an anti-Kerry documentary right before the November 2004 election on the company's sixty-two stations in thirty-nine media markets, was brought to its knees by a web-organized effort to target its national and local advertisers. Already under Wall Street pressure from weak financials, the added pressure from withdrawing advertisers hammered the stock and forced Sinclair to back off its anti-Kerry plans.

This is not to say that all activism begins and ends online—it doesn't. But the online *community* can supplement and complement—and even help finance—the offline activism. In fact, we already have ample evidence of that happening, not just in electoral races, but far beyond that. Consider the protests of Cindy Sheehan in the summer of 2005. Sheehan, whose son, Casey, was killed in the Iraq War, camped out in the oppressive Texas heat near President Bush's ranch in Crawford. Citizen bloggers tracked her trip to Crawford and blogged about her first days in the Texas countryside. Sheehan herself blogged periodically on sites like Daily Kos and the Huffington Post. As her poignant vigil extended into weeks and months, traditional media outlets flocked to her campground to cover the compelling narrative of a grieving mother demanding answers from her president. As the right-wing noise machine attacked her mercilessly, her vigil had a far greater influence on the Iraq War debate than any other antiwar activist or event as of late 2005.

The efforts against Wal-Mart provide another example of modern-day, people-powered activism. Due in large part to the combination of traditional grassroots labor efforts and netroots activism associated with WalmartWatch.com and WakeupWalmart.com, a Zogby poll in November 2005, found unfavorable opinion of Wal-Mart soaring. A large majority of Americans (65 percent) agreed that Wal-Mart had a more negative public image now than compared to the previous year. In contrast, and just as a baseline comparison, only 14 percent of Americans believed that Target's public opinion had worsened in the previous year.

Wakeup Walmart's political director and former Dean For America political director, Paul Blank, told us in June of 2005 about their strategy. "Wal-Mart has to respond if people stop shopping there, right?" Blank asked. "At the end of the day, the reason why we can be so powerful is because we're the ones who shop there. The reason why 3 million people at MoveOn are so powerful is not because it's 3 million people in a country of 300 million. It's because 3 million people organized together. Their ability to influence things is fast and instantaneous, and that's how we're going to change Wal-Mart."

We can expect to see more and more such examples by progressive activists seeking political and societal change. People-powered politics is the decentralization of power from the elites in the media, political, and activism establishments to regular people. Media access and ownership is no longer restricted to the wealthy and connected. Politics, once the playground of machine politicians and the wealthy, is increasingly open to nontraditional candidates, while supporters can now do far more to advocate and support their favorite candidates than volunteer to lick envelopes. And political activism, once the domain of professional organizers and established organizations, has been democratized by new technologies.

Just as significantly, power once concentrated in the political and media centers of this country—Washington D.C., New York City, Los Angeles—has bled out to the rest of the country. Geography is no longer an impediment to participation, as new technologies and the shifting media and political landscapes erase those boundaries. Anyone can participate, from anywhere in the country. No doubt the people-powered phenomenon is still in its infancy, and there is no guarantee that it will survive in the face of increasing government regulation, competition from traditional corporate media outlets, and the ever-present threat of new disruptive technologies.

PARTING LINE

Ask ten people what the Republican Party stands for and you'll get roughly the same ten answers: lower taxes, smaller government, strong national defense, and family values. We can argue about the GOP's fealty to those principles and the ample evidence of hypocrisy, but it's a strong brand born of a very well-defined conservative worldview and set of values. Now ask ten people what the Democratic Party stands for, and you're likely to get ten different answers, many of them *negative*, courtesy of the Republicans that realized that if the Democrats didn't have a brand, they'd offer one up.

When we first set out to write this book, we figured the entire thesis would revolve around the lack of branding and the lack of a coherent vision. As it turned out, this hasn't been a book about policies or new ideas or message, even though those are critically important in taking back our country. We like to believe the ideas that will lead the Democratic Party to a new governing majority already exist, but they need to be articulated clearly.

The book evolved into a much broader discussion of the nascent people-powered mass movement of the netroots and the grassroots, because the progressive message is likely to emerge from there. It has to come collectively from the party rank and file in all fifty states. The hardest movement-building work is happening in the trenches, outside D.C., and those people are the key to the party's future. We have common principles that bind Democrats from places as diverse as Cambridge, Massachusetts, or Madison, Wisconsin, to places like Big Sandy, Montana, or Raleigh, North Carolina. It is those common principles that need to be teased out, packaged, and delivered in wide public forums.

At its core, this new movement is not ideological. There are progressive values that differentiate us from the Republican Party over issues such as privacy, corporate responsibility, foreign policy, and so on. Beyond that, we are pragmatic and believe the Democratic Party has room for a lot of different viewpoints and for individual beliefs and values that might deviate from the party orthodoxy a small percent of the time.

To get to be a real majority, progressives will have to put aside our small differences and focus on the commonality of purpose. If we are divided into our single-issue camps, we'll fail. If we have consultants that are allowed to profit without performance, we'll lose. If the infrastructure of think tanks and training centers and media outlets is not built to compete with that of the conservative machine, we'll start every campaign and debate at a disadvantage.

But we're optimists at heart and we believe that someday we will get past our divisions and our old ways and rebuild our institutions of power. And when we have all that, we will approach ten random people on the street and ask them, "What does the Democratic Party stand for?" and they will all give the same answer.

As we were wrapping up our travels around the country interviewing people, we ended up one day touring Montana governor Brian Schweitzer's ranch (declining an offer to shoot at pesky prairie dogs). We asked him what he would want to hear if people on the street were asked about the Democratic Party.

Schweitzer paused for a bit, then responded with conviction, "They are the party on our side."

But it is going to take more than the Democratic Party slapping that on as a campaign slogan to change the party's image. The party will have to be reformed if it is to remain the primary political vehicle for a populist and progressive movement.[77]

REVOLUTION AND REFORMATION

Even though we have described the obstacles to modernizing the progressive movement—the constituency groups, the consultants who manage the campaigns, and the party establishment itself—our criticisms aren't fueled by significant disagreements of vision. We all want a healthy and effective progressive political agenda enacted into law, and we all want to bury the conservative ideology six feet under. Our criticisms stem from significant differences in how Democrats deal with the ideological agenda of a Republican majority and real disagreements in strategy and tactics designed to win elections. Too many of our progressive brothers and sisters are still taking their cues from their 1970s and 1980s playbooks—which were written when Democrats were a majority in power. The old political hands fear change; the establishment as they knew it is being upended by revolution.

This debate and friction between the old guard and the new movement may get heated at times, but it is good for the Democratic Party and good for the movement. The winning twenty-first-century solutions to the party's ineffectiveness won't come from tweaking twentieth-century tactics. The world has changed far too much for that to work.

The reformation is underway. A whole new generation of progressive activists has stepped in to engage the fight against the conservative juggernaut. We are ready and eager for battle. Technology now allows people from all corners of the country (and even Americans living abroad) to organize and effect change. The netroots is already measured in millions and growing at a terrific pace. By 2005, four to five million progressives were congregating on blogs, while millions more in activist groups were organizing online. It is not inconceivable that we might see these online activist numbers grow to twenty to twenty-five million by the end of the decade.

Being active at the core of this people-powered transformation has been an incredible experience for us, and playing a role in building the infrastructure has been immensely gratifying. But while the media and political elites try to label us as "leaders" in this movement (working off the twentieth-century script where every movement must have clearly defined leaders), the fact is that we are part of a truly organic effort that is decentralized. We are no more "leaders" than anyone else who frequents our websites. We have laid the groundwork and helped build the "public square," but it is the *community* that provides the energy and shapes our agenda.

That's why this movement is so effective—and so threatening to established powers. It is leaderless. It cannot be harnessed, controlled, or co-opted. There is no one to meet in a back room to negotiate a deal. It is a movement that attracts and engages people because it empowers them, not because it gives them yet another flawed "leader" to follow. It returns power where it belongs in a democracy— to the people. In this new movement, people control their own destiny. Throughout history, people have taken hold of such opportunities. Now, we will too.

ACKNOWLEDGMENTS

When we set out to write this book, we had no idea of the sort of commitment we were making in time and energy, and that was time and energy unfairly denied our families. So first and foremost, we owe everything to our wives and children. For Markos, to Elisa and Aristotle. And for Jerome, to Shashi, Taj, and Maya. Also warm and grateful thanks to our parents and siblings.

We thought we knew what it would take to write a book, but we didn't have a clue. We couldn't thank Safir Ahmed enough for his incredible mentorship throughout this writing process. As bloggers we're used to writing three-paragraph blog posts, so putting together nearly 60,000 coherent words didn't come naturally to us. Yet Safir's guidance from beginning to end made a difficult project bearable and made this a far better book. We don't want to consider what this thing would look like without Safir. And while his official title was "editor," he was so much more than that.

Our stock in trade is blogging, and we both run very successful, very busy sites. Yet we were often away from our sites in the process of writing this book. So we owe a big debt of gratitude to the folks who kept them running. At MyDD, Chris Bowers, Scott Shields, Jonathan Singer, and Matt Stoller; and at Daily Kos, Armando, Hunter, Page van der Linden, DavidNYC, and Jeremy Bingham.

We didn't start this book with a clear thesis. We knew we wanted to write about the failures of the Democratic Party and how to reverse them, but our thesis was formulated through discussions with dozens of people all across the country. Few of our preconceived notions survived our research. This book became a distillation of the wisdom of some of the most incredible, passionate, and intelligent people in the world of American politics.

So thanks to all of the following:

In the Midwest: Rick Perlstein in Chicago (and in Milwaukee's Miller Field for a great Brewers game), whose encyclopedic knowledge about the rise of the Goldwater movement is second to none (read his book, *Before the Storm*); Bill Hillsman in Minneapolis, who should go to D.C. and personally kick the ass of every Democratic media consultant; Jeff Blodget in St. Paul of the amazing Wellstone Action; Rick Klau in Chicago; blogger Archpundit in St. Louis; Brad Carson in Tulsa, whom we hope gets back into the electoral game soon enough; and Steve Eichenbaum in Milwaukee, who needs to be better appreciated.

In Montana: Governor Brian Schweitzer, who should someday be president of the United States; Senate President Jon Tester, who belongs in the U.S. Senate, and his awesome wife Sharla; Skip Schloss, who twice gave us a place to stay and arranged the most incredible flight of our lives—from Big Sandy to Whitefish through Glacier National Park; David Sirota, who doesn't seem to have an "off" button; Tom Daubert; Bill Lombardi; blogger Matt Singer; and state legislators Dan Weinberg, Mike Jopek, and Brady Weisman.

In Arizona: Joel Wright in gorgeous Strawberry (definitely worth the drive); and Chris Brown, Rod Pritchett, Raymond Bolger and Steve Tuttle in the Phoenix area, who gave us one of the most entertaining (if depressing) political landscape interviews (turns out there's not much of a Democratic Party in Arizona).

In Colorado: Bobby Clark, who was our guide to the Denver political world; Rick Ridder, Jared Polis, Michael Huttner, Senate President Joan Fitz-Gerald, and Speaker of the House Andrew Romanoff, all of whom helped us understand the remarkable Democratic renaissance in their state.

In Texas: Nathan Wilcox was both a fountain of information about Texas politics and also played the "guide" role; George Strong, Dean Rindy, Glenn Smith, Chuck McDonald, and Jim Moore for the enlightening interviews; bloggers Karl Thomas-Musselman, David Strauss, Mike Nicholson, and Trei Brundrett who are ahead of their time for taking back Texas.

In the Washington, D.C., area: Simon Rosenberg, one of the most solid and tireless allies of the blogosphere inside the capital; Richard Yeselson, our source of first resort for all things related to labor unions; Senator Russ Feingold, Dan Lucas, Ralph Neas, Mark Schmitt, Mike McCurry, Rob Stein, Joe Trippi, Mame Reiley, Amy Sullivan, Walter Ludwig, John Judis, Ruy Teixeira, Mike and Sally Ford, David Brock, Peter Murray, Todd Webster, Paul Blank, Michael Bassik, Matt Bai, Murshed Zaheed, Susan Turnbell, Jennie Blackton, Tony Raymond, Mark Halprin, and Governor Mark Warner (who will be president if Jerome gets his way).

In Philadelphia, which hosts one of the largest netroots communities in the nation: Duncan Black (a.k.a. Atrios).

In New York: The incredible Iara Peng, who would be representing the progressive side in the television gabfests if our movement had its act together; Jamie Daves, who is a point man in the building of a left-wing noise machine; Joe Conason, who is one of our movement's key voices; and Robin McIver and Stuart Elliott for giving us the Madison Avenue view of the world of politics.

In California: Deborah and Andy Rappaport, who seem to be everywhere these days in their tireless efforts to build a VLWC; Dave Johnson, who helped us make sense of the VRWC; Lisa Seitz, Wes Boyd, Joan Blades and George Lakoff, for laying waste to the idea that this book was about message; Amy Kiser and David Brodwin.

In North Carolina: blogger Mathew Gross for providing the rides; Jerry Meek for his southern hospitality and terrific leadership; Zach Ambrose, Morgan Jackson, and Brad Thompson.

Thanks to everyone we talked to on background or off the record. We can't thank them by name, but they know who they are. As to those we have inevitably failed to mention, we hang our head in shame. We obviously thank them as well.

Thanks to our publisher, Chelsea Green, for being so cool throughout the whole process. We had every opportunity to publish with a big corporate publisher and get a nice fat advance, yet we never regretted our decision to stay with an independent publisher. Thanks to Margo Baldwin for believing big in us, and Jennifer Nix for (among other things) the awesome cabin stay on Beaver Island. Along with Safir, they almost made this book-writing process—dare we say it?—fun. Thanks to Working Assets for working with us to help build and promote the progressive infrastructure. Miles Kurland, whom we've worked with since the Howard Dean campaign days, designed our cover after three book designers failed at the task. He nailed it on the first try, too.

Thanks to every blogger who is turning the promise of people-powered media into reality. The media landscape has changed, and as a result, politics are being affected in ways that no one could have imagined even three or four years ago. Without blogging tools like Blogger, MovableType, and Scoop (thanks Rusty Foster), there would be no easy way to get our words in print. And we shudder to think of a world without Google. It sure wouldn't include this book or our blogs.

But most importantly, bloggers would be lonely, irrelevant voices in the wilderness without the support of our enthusiastic readers, whom we watched grow in number from the hundreds in 2002 to the millions today. So to them we owe everything. This is their book. We may be offering the tools, but it is they who will change the world. Our biggest victories lie ahead of us.

There's one final story from Montana we must share: We ran across a retired rocket scientist named Jim who had spent his entire life designing weapons systems in the California desert. Everyone in the neighborhood thought he was a Republican when we gathered one evening at Skip's house for dinner. "Democrats make me ashamed to be an American," he began, seemingly confirming the suspicions of his partisan leanings. But after a brief pause, he delivered an unexpected punch line: "But Republicans make me ashamed to be a human being."

So thanks to Jim and his wife Marion, because they fed Jerome blueberry pancakes as Markos slept in.

NOTES

1. Michael S. Gerber, "Former Bush Adviser 'Consulting' for KBR," *The Examiner* (Washington, DC), March 22, 2005, http://www.dcexaminer.com/articles/2005/03/22/news/d_c_news/02newsdc23kkr.txt.

2. Halliburton Watch, "Halliburton Gets Katrina Contract, Hires Former FEMA Director," September 1, 2005, http://www.halliburtonwatch.org/news/hurricane_katrina.html.

3. Jim VandeHei, "Blueprint Calls for Bigger, More Powerful Government," *Washington Post*, February 9, 2005, p. A01, http://www.washingtonpost.com/wp-dyn/articles/A9307-2005Feb8.html.

4. Greg Botelho, "Small Inroads Make Difference for Bush," CNN.com, November 4, 2004, http://www.cnn.com/2004/ALLPOLITICS/11/03/prez.key/.

5. Patrick J. Buchanan, "A National Emergency," WorldNet Daily, August 29, 2005, http://www.worldnetdaily.com/news/article.asp?ARTICLE_ID=46019.

6. Arianna Huffington, "President Bush Hits the Scene, Giving Hope to… Uh, Trent Lott," The Huffington Post, September 2, 2005, http://www.huffingtonpost.com/arianna-huffington/president-bush-hits-the-s_b_6670.html.

7. Michael D. Brown and others, digitally scanned email messages, http://i.a.cnn.net/cnn/2005/images/11/03/brown.emails.pdf.

8. *New York Times*, "Barbara Bush Calls Evacuees Better Off," September 7, 2005, http://www.nytimes.com/2005/09/07/national/nationalspecial/07barbara.html?ex=1135141200&en=5fe3b290dcdc2f7b&ei=5070.

9. Purva Patel, "Delay to Evacuees: 'Is This Kind of Fun?'" DomeBlog (*The Houston Chronicle*), September 9, 2005, http://blogs.chron.com/domeblog/archives/2005/09/delay_to_evacue.html.

10. Massimo Calabresi, "Looking for a Corpse to Make a Case," *Time* (online edition), September 17, 2005, http://www.time.com/time/nation/article/0,8599,1106213,00.html.

11. Alan Cooperman, "Where Most See a Weather System, Some See Divine Retribution," *Washington Post*, September 4, 2005, p. A27, http://www.washingtonpost.com/wp-dyn/content/article/2005/09/03/AR2005090301408.html.

12. Rick Scarborough, "New Orleans—When God Opens the Floodgates," The Rick Scarborough Report on the War on Faith (e-newsletter) 1:24, September 2, 2005, http://www.visionamerica.us/site/DocServer/rsr0124.pdf?docID=212.

13. Institute of Government Studies Library, University of California (Berkeley), "Proposition 75: Use of Union Dues for Political Purposes," http://www.igs.berkeley.edu/library/htUnionDues.html.

14. House Judiciary Committee Democratic Staff, "Preserving Democracy: What Went Wrong in Ohio (Executive Summary)," Truthout.org, January 5, 2005, http://www.truthout.org/docs_05/010605Y.shtml.

15. Tom Curry, "Democrats Woo Abortion Opponents for Senate," MSNBC.com, March 11, 2005, http://www.msnbc.msn.com/id/7150734/.

16. NARAL Pro-Choice America, "Justice Janice Rogers Brown," July 2003, http://www.prochoiceamerica.org/facts/jbrown_facts.cfm.

17. Adele M. Stan, "Power Preying," *Mother Jones*, November/December 1995, http://www.motherjones.com/news/feature/1995/11/stan.html.

18. Institute for First Amendment Studies, "Religious Right Update," *Freedom Writer*, April 1995, http://www.publiceye.org/ifas/fw/9504/update.html.

19. David Plotz, "Ralph Reed's Creed," Slate, May 4, 1997, http://slate.msn.com/id/1819.

20. Natural Resources Defense Council, "The Bush Record," http://www.nrdc.org/bushrecord/.

21. Committee on Government Reform—Minority Staff Special Investigations Division and Office of Senator Barbara Boxer Environmental Staff, "Human Pesticide Experiments," June 2005, http://boxer.senate.gov/news/pesticidereport.pdf.

22. Employment Policy Foundation, "Fact & Fallacy: Updating the Reasons for Union Decline," Figure 1, May 1998, http://www.epf.org/pubs/images/ff4-5-1.gif.

23. Bureau of Labor Statistics, Current Population Survey, "Union Members in 2004," January 27, 2005, ftp://ftp.bls.gov/pub/news.release/union2.txt.

24. Liza Featherstone, "Will Labor Take the Wal-Mart Challenge?" *The Nation*, June 10, 2004, http://www.thenation.com/doc/20040628/featherstone.

25. CNN/Money, "Wal-Mart Tops Fortune 500," April 12, 2005, http://money.cnn.com/2005/04/04/news/fortune500/newlist2005/.

26. Timothy Noah, "The Wal-Mart Manifesto," Slate, February 24, 2005, http://slate.msn.com/id/2113954/.

27. United Food and Commercial Workers, "Wal-Mart's Anti-Union Campaign," http://www.ufcw.org/issues_and_actions/walmart_workers_campaign_info/relevant_links/anti_union_manuals.cfm.

28. Center for Responsive Politics, "2004 Election Overview: Business-Labor-Ideology Split in PAC & Individual Donations to Candidates and Parties," http://www.opensecrets.org/overview/blio.asp?cycle=2004.

29. Election-day poll by Peter D. Hart Research Associates for the AFL-CIO.

30. *Patriot News* (Harrisburg, PA), "Pro-choice and women's groups still angry," June 9, 2005.

31. National Council of Women's Organizations, "The ABCs of Women's Issues," http://www.womensorganizations.org/pdfs/abcs.pdf.

32. Survey USA, "Pro-live vs. Pro-choice," September 12, 2005, http://www.surveyusa.com/50state2005/50StateAbortion0805SortedbyProLife.htm.

33. Arianna Huffington, "The Governor's Race and the Rain Dance," Arianna Online, June 5, 1998, http://ariannaonline.com/columns/column.php?id=448.

34. Thomas B. Edsall and James V. Grimaldi, "On Nov. 2, GOP Got More for Its Billion, Analysis Shows," *Washington Post*, December 30, 2004, p. A01, http://www.washingtonpost.com/wp-dyn/articles/A35062-2004Dec29.html

35. Paul Farhi, "Campaign Ads Enrich Advisors," MSNBC.com, February 10, 2004, http://msnbc.msn.com/id/4226901/.

36. Ryan Lizza, "The Ad War '04," *New York*, April 19, 2003, http://newyorkmetro.com/nymetro/news/politics/national/2004race/adwars/n_10182/index1.html.

37. View the ad at http://www.dailykos.com/Banderas.mpg.

38. Tyler Bridges, "Florida GOP Aims Big TV Ad Campaign at Hispanics," *Puerto Rico Herald*, July 4, 2002, http://www.puertorico-herald.org/issues/2002/vol6n28/FLGopAims-en.shtml.

39. The (Harvard University) Institute of Politics, John F. Kennedy School of Government, and Harvard University, *Campaign for President: The Managers Look at 2004*, (Lanham, MD: Rowman & Littlefield, 2005), p. 224.

40. Max Blumenthal, "Hitler in Virginia," *The Nation*, October 26, 2005, http://www.thenation.com/docprint.mhtml?i=20051107&s=blumenthal.

41. Robert Barnes, "Ads May Hurt Kilgore More Than They Help," *Washington Post*, October 30, 2005, p. A11, http://www.washingtonpost.com/wp-dyn/content/article/2005/10/29/AR2005102901378.html.

42. Ibid.

43. Joe Cappo, *The Future of Advertising: New Media, New Clients, New Consumers in the Post-Television Age*, (New York: McGraw-Hill, 2003).

44. New Politics Institute, "Fundamental Shifts in the U.S. Media and Advertising Industries," November 2005, http://www.ndnpac.org/pdfs/ShiftsinMediaandAdvertising.pdf.

45. Saul Hansell, "It's Not TV, It's Yahoo," *New York Times*, September 24, 2005, http://www.nytimes.com.

46. Jupiter Research, "Marketing and Branding Forecast," *Marketing and Branding*, Vol. 3, 2003, http://www.dallasnews.com/mediakit/audience/industry_research/images/jupiter_2.pdf

47. *Campaign for President.*

48. Ibid.

49. Ibid.

50. Dan Balz, "Democrats' Grass Roots Shift the Power," *Washington Post*, February 20, 2005, p. A04, http://www.washingtonpost.com/wp-dyn/articles/A38436-2005Feb19.html.

51. David C. Johnson, "Appendix 2: An Example of Interconnectedness" in *The Attack on Trial Lawyers and Tort Law*, (Menlo Park, CA: The Commonweal Institute, October 1, 2003), http://commonwealinstitute.org/reports/tort/Appendix2.html.

52. Brian Montopoli, "It's a Pig, Any Way You Look at It," *CJR Daily*, January 14, 2005, http://www.cjrdaily.org/archives/001242.asp.

53. Chris Bowers, "Dailykos Is As Large As the Entire Conservative Blogosphere," MyDD, September 9, 2005, http://www.mydd.com/story/2005/9/9/2265/71257.

54. Other funders include the F.M. Kirby Foundation, the Lynde and Harry Bradley Foundation, and the Richard and Helen DeVos Foundation. Media Transparency, "Recipient Grants: Leadership Institute," http://www.mediatransparency.org/recipientgrants.php?600.

55. Jordan Robertson, "Coach Approach: More Firms Employ Mentors to Groom Rising Executives," *Dallas Morning News*, August 17, 2005, http://www.dallasnews.com.

56. Ethics and Public Policy Center, "Naomi Schaefer Riley," http://www.eppc.org/scholars/scholarID.67/scholar.asp.

57. Center for Responsive Politics, "2004 Election Overview: Stats at a Glance," http://www.opensecrets.org/overview/stats.asp?cycle=2004.

58. N. C., "Savage on 'Billionaire George Goebbels Soros': 'A Money Changer in the Temple of Truth'," Media Matters for America, June 8, 2004, http://mediamatters.org/items/200406080004.

59. A. S., "On FOX, Tony Blankley Called Soros 'A Jew Who Figured Out a Way to Survive the Holocaust'," Media Matters for America, June 4, 2004, http://mediamatters.org/items/200406040004.

60. Center for Responsive Politics, "527s: America Coming Together, 2004 Election Cycle," http://www.opensecrets.org/527s/527events.asp?orgid=10.

61. James Harding, "Soros Group Raises Stakes in Battle with Neo-Cons," Truthout.org (reprinted from *Financial Times*), January 11, 2005, http://www.truthout.org/docs_05/011305W.shtml.

62. Hans Nichols, "Soros Says Be Patient," *The Hill*, April 20, 2005, http://www.hillnews.com/thehill/export/TheHill/News/Frontpage/042005/soros.html. The article refers to "Phoenix Group." That was the working name for the Stein group before it settled on "Democracy Alliance."

63. Paul Farhi, "Small Donors Grow Into Big Political Force," *Washington Post*, May 3, 2004, p. A01.

64. Roll Call, "Heard on the Hill," July 22, 2002.

65. Al From and Bruce Reed, "DLC Memo: The Real Soul of the Democratic Party," Democratic Leadership Council, May 15, 2003, http://www.dlc.org/ndol_ci.cfm?contentid=251690&kaid=127&subid=900056.

66. Ryan Lizza, "Campaign Journal: Dean.com," New Republic, May 23, 2003, http://www.tnr.com/doc.mhtml?pt=MsFThRpEfeVRNVf9ei9j2R.

67. Charles Lewis, "Political Mugging in America," Center for Public Integrity, March 4, 2004, http://www.publicintegrity.org/report.aspx?aid=194&sid=200.

68. Annatopia.com, "The Truth About Martin Frost, Part Two," January 19, 2005, http://annatopia.com/archives/001064.html.

69. Chris Bowers, "More on Roemer," MyDD, January 9, 2005, http://www.mydd.com/story/2005/1/9/14148/95794.

70. Mark Warner, "Winning Back the White House," Forward Together Political Action Committee, Summer 2005, http://www.forwardtogetherpac.com/php-bin/news/showArticle.php?id=10.

71. Chris Bowers, "Uncontested," MyDD, November 5, 2004, http://www.mydd.com/story/2004/11/5/115834/784.

72. Center for Responsive Politics, "Congressional Races: Total Raised and Spent: 2004 Race: Texas District 22," http://www.opensecrets.org/races/summary.asp?ID=TX22&Cycle=2004.

73. Chris Bowers, "What to Look for Tonight," MyDD, August 2, 2005, http://www.mydd.com/story/2005/8/2/143725/9524.

74. Dan Balz and Thomas B. Edsall, "Gingrich Says Ohio Race Holds Lesson for GOP," *Washington Post*, August 4, 2005, p. A04, http://www.washingtonpost.com/wp-dyn/content/article/2005/08/03/AR2005080301899.html.

75. Democratic Legislative Campaign Committee, "The DLCC's Long-Term Plan: For the Third Election in a Row, Democratic Legislators See Net Gains on Election Night," November 9, 2005, http://www.dlcc.org/news/2005_successes.html.

76. Thomas Ferguson and Joel Rogers, *Right Turn: The Decline of the Democrats and the Future of American Politics* (New York: Hill & Wang, 1986), p. 199.

77. For an explanation of what we mean by *progressive*, we refer the reader to "What is Progressive?" by Andrew Garib, http://www.alternet.org/wiretap/23706/, and "Progressivism in 2004: Transcending the Liberal-Conservative Divide," by John Halpin, http://www.americanprogress.org/site/pp.asp?c=biJRJ8OVF&b=18188.

INDEX

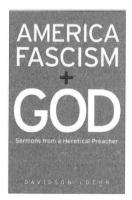
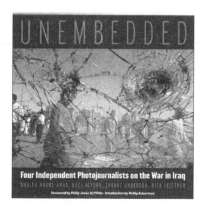